Richmond upon Thames Libraries

Renew online at www.richmond.gov.uk/libraries

PROVOCATIONS

IN DEFENCE OF POLITICAL CORRECTNESS

YASMIN ALIBHAI-BROWN

SERIES EDITOR:

YASMIN ALIBHAI-BROWN

\Bᵇ\
Biteback Publishing

First published in Great Britain in 2018 by
Biteback Publishing Ltd
Westminster Tower
3 Albert Embankment
London SE1 7SP

ISBN 978-1-78590-414-1

10 9 8 7 6 5 4 3 2 1

A CIP catalogue record for this book is available from the British Library.

Set in Stempel Garamond

Printed and bound in Great Britain by

CPI Group (UK) Ltd, Croydon CR0 4YY

When blows have made me stay, I fled from words.

Coriolanus, ACT II SCENE II

Abuses of our freedoms of expression ... tear apart a society, brutalize its dominant elements, and persecute, even to extermination, its minorities.

JUSTICE JACKSON, US SUPREME COURT JUDGE

The one freedom they seem to truly care about is the freedom to incite bigotry; this freedom trumps the freedom of minorities to live unencumbered by prejudice, threats to personal safety, and discrimination ... Perversely it is these right-wing abusers of 'free speech' who are the most chronically offended ... [They] are offended by critiques of privilege, attempts to come to terms with the past, or simply ideas that challenge injustice.

OWEN JONES, THE GUARDIAN

The best lack all conviction, while the worst Are full of passionate intensity.

W. B. YEATS, 'THE SECOND COMING'

Contents

Introduction

IS POLITICAL CORRECTNESS (PC) a modern blight or a blessing? A neo-communist undertaking or a virtuous moral code? Is it unbelievable stupidity, a veritable threat to freedom, pathetic weakness or necessary disruption?

Believers, agnostics and detractors fundamentally disagree about what PC is, the harm or good it does and its place in a liberal democracy. However, all sides agree that PC is potent, puissant, heady. It excites and enrages us. It provokes discord and derision, it stirs things up and promises – or portends – radical change. Millions of words have been written on this subject over the decades, and more stream out all the time, continuing to split and rupture populations, communities, families, friends and lovers.

The confrontation between advocates of uninhibited

communication and those who believe in self-restraint and fairness has gone on for several decades. But now, one side has decided to fight dirty, to purge the opposition. A multitude of websites and conservatives (with a small 'c') issue siren warnings about repressive thought and speech controllers, the new generation of Stalinists and Maoists. Facts are doctored; arguments scorned. These are closed fraternities, torrid, full of furies and complaints. *They want their world back.*

These warriors feel persecuted or endangered all the time. Sad really. They got agitated because cartoon bad boy Dennis the Menace is no longer as horrible as he once was. When the character was rightly toned down by pub lishers in 2008 and the BBC in 2017, traditionalists were awfully vexed. They stamped their feet. They wanted their gnashing young bully back. Similar indignation broke out when Jodie Whittaker, a *woman*, was chosen to play Doctor Who in July 2017. New complaints pour in every day. And fantastical contentions too. Martin Daubney, erstwhile editor of *Loaded* magazine, warned in 2017: 'London is becoming a global laughing stock. Both intellectually and literally, Londoners are dying under the weight of a virulent dose of political correctness.'[1] Such alarmists need to be taken seriously, very seriously. They are mighty influencers in today's fragmented and divided world.

The war of the words can be whipped up in an instant. Let us remember the woeful furore over the Cadbury Easter egg hunt in the spring of 2017. Some mischief makers put it about that the word 'Easter' had been removed from the publicity for the annual children's event. Not so, said Cadbury and the National Trust, who organised the event. They had changed one sentence to attract people of all faiths to the egg hunt; 'Easter' was still blazoned on the National Trust website. Cadbury and the charity were not trying to expunge Christ's foundational story. Even so, anti-PC flames could not be contained. By then, a bogus accusation had more traction than the truth, as so often happens. The Archbishop of York, John Sentamu, grimly accused the organisers of spitting on the grave of John Cadbury, founder of the family firm. The family were, in fact, Quakers. And, as Quakers do not mark Easter, the long-dead Mr Cadbury

1   Martin Daubney, 'Politically Correct London is Becoming a Global Laughing Stock', DPC website: https://atnnow.com/dpc/politically-correct-london-becoming-global-laughing-stock/

will not be restive in his grave over this manufactured crisis. Theresa May, on her way to trade talks in the Middle East, condemned the airbrushing of faith from Easter. Who exactly was doing that, pray? Corbyn joined the fray, and confessed he too was upset by the way the company had behaved. The subtext was, as ever, cultural protectionism. 'Real' Britain was being blitzed by 'multiculturalists' and Muslims, who are all on a perpetual jihad. And godless white liberals. Meanwhile, a parcel had arrived for me at home. It contained a smashed Easter egg and a crucifix drawn on a scrappy piece of paper. No address, no name. Message understood. Is this acceptable? Is it even sane?

Within the Anglo-Saxon axis, anti-political correctness has gone mad, bad and treacherous too. Invective, lies, hate speech, bullying, intemperance and prejudices have become the new norms. Intolerable deeds are justified through invocations of liberty. Restraint is oppression. Anything goes. Freedom of speech and freedom of expression are weaponised. Trump and Farage have tapped into the worst of human nature and whipped up nativist populism and political toxicity. It is done with charm, humour, phoney humility and invocations to the common man and woman.

As Salman Rushdie observes in his 2017 novel *The Golden House*, which is set in a modern America that is chaotic, amoral and dystopian; a place where millions voted in a boorish, sexually feral, unpredictable President:

> What was astonishing, what made this election like no other was that people backed him *because* he was insane, not in spite of it … Sikh taxi drivers and rodeo cowboys, rabid alt-right blondes and black brain surgeons agreed, we love his craziness, no milquetoast euphemisms from him, he shoots straight from the hip, says what he fucking well wants to say … he's our guy'.[2]

A meticulously researched, disturbing article in the *Observer Magazine* shed light on the way freedom is now exploited by those who most proclaim it. Backpage. com was America's second largest classified ad website. One mother, Kubiiki Pride, used it to get second-hand goods. Then, in 2009, her thirteen-year-old daughter disappeared. After nine months of unimaginable agony, her

---

2   Salman Rushdie, *The Golden House* (Jonathan Cape, 2017).

husband suggested that they should look for her on Back-page. Pride was incredulous: 'I thought it was a site where you bought and sold stuff … It never occurred to me that children were being bought and sold, too.' She clicked on the adult section, and there she saw her thirteen-year-old daughter, almost naked, posing invitingly. She had been snatched by a trafficker, beaten, given drugs, broken and then sold. They found her and brought her home. Her torturer was imprisoned. But the publishers and editors at Backpage refused to take down the image. According to the US National Centre for Missing and Exploited Children, the number of such cases has gone up by 846 per cent since 2010, mainly because the internet is ungov-erned and ungovernable. Several judges concluded that Backpage was not accountable because, under US law, internet companies have immunity for content posted by third parties. It was only in 2017 that affected fami-lies were able to take out civil suits against the publishers.

The men who own the business see themselves as upholders of non-negotiable freedoms. At long last, in 2016, these amoral millionaires were called before a Senate sub-committee. That day they closed down the adult listings on the website. Two of them published this statement: 'Today, the censors prevailed ... [This] is an assault on the First Amendment. We maintain hope for a more robust and unbowed internet in the future.'[3]

Are these fiends or men? They are men who have fiendish notions of rights and liberties. They use their power and the US constitution to do what they damn well please. In Greek mythology, Hades was the supreme, cruel god of the underworld. He also abducted pretty young maidens like Persephone. She was picking flowers when Hades pulled her into the dark depths of earth. Contemporary libertarianism has turned our world as dark and fetid as Hades's grim kingdom.

But isn't the UK more moderate, less extreme? No. There was once a civilised consensus about sensible, flexible limits to what was acceptable in public discourse. However, Steve Bannon, godfather of the hard-right website, Breitbart, Arron Banks, co-owner of West-monster.com (wicked little brother of Breitbart), Nigel Farage and other hard nationalists have driven their 'free

---

3   Annie Kelly, *Observer Magazine*, 2 July 2017.

speech' tanks over that consensus to establish a new order where racism, sexism, homophobia, xenophobia and abuse are proudly expressed. Behemoths like the BBC are weak and querulous before these cowboys. Our world is changed – and absolutely not for the better.

Good people have been inert for too long while this malevolence was diffused through society. The new barbarians must be pushed back. The time feels right. In May 2017, two libertarian idols, Kelvin MacKenzie and Katie Hopkins, were pushed off the belfries from where they regularly rang their loud anti-PC bells. MacKenzie was sacked by *The Sun*, after he wrote a column about Chelsea and England footballer Ross Barkley, who is mixed race and thoroughly British. Barkley, who had been punched in a pub for no good reason, reminded Mr MacKenzie of a 'gorilla'. Ms Hopkins, a mordant, attention-seeking columnist for the MailOnline presented a live phone-in show on LBC on which she quickly became a heroine to the libertarian right. She was outspoken, provocative, rude and nasty, mostly to those on the left and minorities. After a Muslim suicide bomber killed twenty-two children and adults in

Manchester, Ms Hopkins called for a 'final solution' in a tweet. The radio station terminated her contract because those words evoke memories of the Holocaust. Her bosses sat back while she insulted and abused Muslims, black people, the poor – ratings were what mattered. But those two words did it for her. And four words: 'letter boxes' and 'bank robbers', caused a quake both across the nation and within the Tory Party. In his *Daily Telegraph* column, Boris Johnson used the terms to deride fully veiled Muslim women. A large number of Britons were offended, while others backed his candour. Theresa May proclaimed, 'It's imperative that everybody is careful in the language that they use.' She called on him to apologise. The erstwhile Foreign Secretary remained defiant and went on holiday. You see, there is no total freedom of speech, and a very good thing, too.[4] Most disputes and claims about 'censorship' are phoney.

Charlie Gere is an esteemed professor of media theory and history at Lancaster University. His reflections on liberty and restraint are incontrovertible: 'There

---

4   I borrow this from a persuasive book, *There's no Such Thing as Free Speech: And It's A Good Thing Too* (OUP, 1994) by American law professor Stanley Fish.

are rather just degrees of tolerance, permissiveness and relative freedom, with boundaries, legal, social and cultural. And there are always limits, many of which we are barely aware of, so much do we take them for granted.'[5]

I sense an observable change in the weatherglass and the atmosphere. In our era of unregulated internet traffic, Britons are now more concerned about the dangers of untrammelled communication, and social Darwinism. This may be just my own fierce optimism of the will, but I see the shadow of something approaching, a transformative momentum. Or at least an emerging understanding that social responsibility matters as much as individual rights. As with all significant societal shifts, resistors are also regrouping and rebooting. The divide is not along political lines; defenders and attackers can be of the right and left, traditionalists or liberals.

Although people of all persuasions are beginning to get uneasy about verbal violence and power inequalities, those who dread or disparage PC get more attention and respect than those who stand up for the concept and its

---

5   Letter in *The Guardian*, 1 October 2008.

impact. This means that there is payoff for being anti-PC and even better rewards for the converts, PC proponents who see the light and denounce their previous selves.[6]

For all its many flaws and idiocies,[7] PC fosters civility between diverse humans and tames the beast within each and every one of us. Without PC, the social environment becomes coarse and contaminated. The law of the jungle prevails, ensures that only the strongest and cruellest survive. Britain has become edgy, tense, unfair, unequal, scrappy, eruptive and disjointed. Surely no one can feel safe and happy in such an environment?

Truth be told, the politically correct are also to blame for the state we are in. We have been weak and risibly ineffective. We allowed the enemy to capture too much territory. We were laid low by counterattacks and slurs. When the going gets tough, the tough should get going, with conviction and integrity. We didn't do that.

We should have been more assured and sharp. We

---

6   Trevor Phillips, a black Briton, made Channel 4 programme *Has PC Gone Mad?*, which started with his own conversion. The programme enhanced his reputation as a 'freethinker' and an honest broker.

7   The anti-PC brigade has its own flaws and idiocies, passed off as 'common sense'.

should have defended the ideals embodied in this credo. We should also have claimed credit for ensuring truly obnoxious statements and behaviours have become unacceptable. There have been many instances of individuals who were forced, by public anger, to withdraw iniquitous remarks and to apologise. Every time this happened, we should have pointed out that this was political correctness at work, cleaning up verbal litter and foulness in our joint, common habitats. Health and safety rules have made citizens, well, safer than they have ever been. As ever, there are always examples of foolish excesses, but should schools let kids climb up big trees without supervision and learn lessons through falling? Again, I do not believe Britons really want harassment or abuse to proliferate unchecked. Workplaces where sexism and racism are not tolerated are better for all employees and bosses, even the compulsive lech. In one debate I took part in, a Tory told me PC had destroyed male–female relationships. He is the father of many girls. I asked him what he would do if his daughter was leered at, touched, pinched or grabbed by strange men on her way to work: 'I'd take my gun and shoot the buggers.' Oh, so PC after all.

I commissioned the indomitable Claire Fox to write *'I Find That Offensive!'* for this series. It is a sharp polemic against 'censorship', squeamishness and PC. At the book launch I said that though I disagreed with almost every word, her arguments were interesting and robust. This is my considered, emotional (as well as rational) response to Fox and others leading the charge against PC. In her book, Fox described taking part in a school debate on Ched Evans, the convicted rapist. Should he be allowed to play professional football again? During the Q&A, she said rape was 'not necessarily the worst thing that could ever happen to an individual'. The pupils and teachers were 'shell-shocked'. So, frankly, was I. Since 2010, various studies by reputable organisations have found that young men do not understand consent and do not think non-consensual sex is rape. A detailed NSPCC/Bristol University study found that three quarters of girls interviewed had experienced emotional aggression from sexual partners, a third had suffered sexual violence and of those one in ten reported severe violence. In higher education institutions sexual violations are endemic. Teachers and university academic staff are trying to re-educate sexually aggressive males, many of whom are also accessing violent porn online. I do not think Fox's possibly throwaway words led to sexual assaults. But they did diminish the seriousness of a very serious crime.

Fox also defends trolls who attack females in public spaces – even Milo Yiannopoulos, the hard right, Breitbart 'provocateur' who freely shared vile racist and sexist thoughts, until he (allegedly) backed adult sex with underage children. Then the golden boy of the hard right fell to earth.

Words, I believe hurt, wound, incapacitate and cause mental distress. Worse than all of that, they intimidate and silence certain voices. The uncivil and brutish have weaponised freedom of speech. Large numbers of talented and exceptional people are now too frightened to speak up. Libertarians see that as contemptible weakness. To be human is to be vulnerable and sensitive. That is what I would dearly like Claire Fox and her ideological kith and kin to think about and understand.

As this book was being written, Harvey Weinstein, the Hollywood mogul, was pulled down from his ivory tower. Several female actresses – a number of them young

– led the way, alongside Ashley Judd, Rose McGowan, Mira Sorvino, Asia Argento and Ambra Battilana Gutierrez, who even reported him to NYPD and secretly recorded his advances. Dozens more followed, including top stars Angelina Jolie and Gwyneth Paltrow. So are these weaklings and perpetual moaners who can't survive male advances? Or maybe just another batch of 'snowflakes'?

These were repulsive acts committed by an all-powerful, controlling man. But what stopped the women from coming out were his words – words that scared them, made them feel they had to comply.

Words and deeds cannot be neatly kept apart; words can cause deeds. At times, words can also hurt more than actions. And words do not float around in a void. They connect us to lived realities, to each other. Language and communication affects well-being, psychological stability, relationships, sense of belonging and cohesion. Families break up, people commit suicide and neighbourhoods turn deadly when intemperate words are used without due care. Sara, a young mentee of mine, is sixteen, mixed race and very bright. Her skin is light, her hair brown and afro. Verbal bullying in school and online has turned her into an almost silent, introverted, frightened, housebound, self-harming creature. She has been called a 'mongrel' and a 'half-monkey'. Twice she's been slapped in the playground. Slaps, she says, hurt less than the daily verbal stings. She has tried to bleach off the blackness on her arms, ending up in blisters. In 2017, a young Indian couple I had befriended, abruptly returned to India before completing their employment contracts. They were both gifted designers, who had been brought over to London by British companies. They explained that though they loved London and their jobs, the murmur of intolerance and racist banter in their workplace had been too much to bear. Their idea of England has been shaken. They would never come back.

Encouragingly, some men and women, who previously championed freedom of expression as if it was a sacred doctrine, are now listening and, at least thinking, about what should be off-limits. Journalist and bestselling author Dolly Alderton is one of them. At the Edinburgh Fringe, she went to a comedy gig. Reginald D. Hunter was on. She loved his humour. But a fun night turned into something else: 'That night ... he came on stage to perform a bizarrely sexist set, continuingly referring to women as "bitches", claiming misogyny didn't exist and making extraordinarily sweeping statements about female immorality.' For the first time in her life, she heckled, told whoever would listen that he should not be allowed a platform. She is not and will never be PC in the way I am. But her reactions three years ago show she understands the impact words have on our lives and our world.[8]

I am a freethinking writer who believes sticks and stones can break bones, but words can break your will. In November 2016, I was spat at by a middle-aged white woman in London, on a bus on High Street Kensington. She also verbally abused me and told me to go back to where I came from. The spit was easily wiped off. Her words still hurt. After forty-five years, in just a few seconds, a nobody took away my sense of place. How is this acceptable? Is this what we want in our multiracial, multifarious democracy? Those who breezily say such hurt is

---

8 'Dolly Alderton on Whether Political Correctness is Changing Comedy', *Sunday Times Style Magazine*, 22 July 2018.

a price worth paying tend to be white, middle class, heterosexual and secure. They cannot understand what it is like not to be white, middle class, heterosexual or secure.

Liberty is one of the most precious of human rights. I was born and raised in Uganda, where there was no real freedom of speech – not when it was a British protectorate, not when it became an independent country and absolutely not under Idi Amin's military dictatorship. After I was exiled to Britain in 1972 I was finally able to think and speak without fear. But liberty is neither anarchy, nor licence to degrade and destroy. Furthermore, censorship by the powerful is not the same as sensitive, considerate communication. Equality policies are not creeping communism; fairness and dignity are not revolutionary aims. The most ardent free speech warrior meekly accepts state secretiveness, libel laws, injunctions against Holocaust denial and intrusions into the royal family.

As I finish writing this polemic, the Labour Party is engulfed in an almighty, long-running dispute with a large section of the British Jewish population. Jeremy Corbyn and his policymakers stand accused of anti-Semitism because they have decided not to accept the International Holocaust

Remembrance Alliance's (IHRA) definition of the term, as they have serious reservations about the wording. Their opponents are furious and insist this reluctance indicates deep anti-Semitism. However, myself and many others, including top British Jewish legal experts such as Sir Geoffrey Bindman and ex-High Court judge Stephen Sedley, are uncomfortable about the definition because it could lead to a suppression of legitimate debate about some of Israel's policies and actions in Palestinian and occupied territories.[9]

In 2017, a large group of professors wrote a joint letter that was published in *The Guardian*:

> The government has 'adopted' the International Holocaust Remembrance Alliance definition of antisemitism, which can be and is being read as extending to criticism of Israel and support for Palestinian rights, an entirely separate issue, as prima facie evidence of antisemitism. This definition seeks to conflate criticism of Israel with antisemitism.

In 2017 Jo Johnson, the erstwhile minister for Universities

---

9   See my column in *i*, 1 August 2018.

and Science, instructed universities to adopt a definition of anti-Semitism, which could potentially supress debates about Israeli policies. This was censorship. Universities, we are always told by the right, should be open to all views. The mantra was often repeated by Jo Johnson. But Israel, it seems, gets special protection. Imagine how British Muslim students feel about the double standards.

These same people who say they uphold freedom of expression also vocally support the curtailing of free debates on Israel and Palestine. The clash between the Labour Party and the Board of Deputies of British Jews raises difficult questions. Should people be able to say what they wish in public spaces? Or do they have to be aware that words have meanings, histories and tremendous power to bring about consequences? Do citizens in liberal societies have the right to talk to extremists or those outside the social and political consensus? Or do they have to be careful about what they say and who they interact with? The conflicts, tensions and contradictions are playing out dramatically. This is a PC conflict writ large.

In 2013 I wrote, 'Freedom of expression in the West is hokum, I say. It's hypocrisy dressed up as high virtue

... The internet is almost absolutely free and look how ugly and frightening that space is becoming. Imagine all that poison coursing through the real world.' That's what has happened and now our human bonds are being corroded.[10] The fractious, wild web has corrupted real, lived bonds between humans. You can see how across the UK. Men, women and children are unhappier and more mentally distressed than they have ever been.[11]

For Margaret Thatcher there was no such thing as society. She was wrong. Humans are social beings. Unlike most other animals we form bonds with those outside our family and ethnic groups. More remarkably, we learn to accommodate (not rip into or eat) those who are different. This is only possible if we temper our instinctive feelings and behaviours. No collective human group would survive if each member spoke without any self-control or moderation or care. PC, at its best, is sensitivity to the feelings and needs of others and also fair

---

10 *The Independent*, 24 September 2012.

11 See research by the Mental Health Foundation, published in May 2017, which showed that two thirds of Britons have suffered from mental ill health. Our figures are higher than many developed nations and getting worse.

power sharing. 'Do unto others as you would have them do unto you', said Jesus in his Sermon on the Mount. You could say PC is a nobly Christian doctrine.

Some months after Brexit, a right-wing journalist who wanted out of Europe confided he was feeling a bit wretched even though his side had won the referendum. He voted to leave because he is against regulations imposed by states or international bodies, particularly on small businesses. But, as we know, the referendum was used by UKIP and other nationalists to whip up atrocious anti-immigrant feeling. Some radio and TV programmes were turned into bear pits. My journalist friend now sees the noxious side effects of the campaign: 'This is not a country I recognise. This is rude and boorish. We English are polite people. It's one of our strongest cultural traits. How do we get that back?' This man never knowingly described himself as PC but he clearly grew accustomed to certain codes of language and behaviour in his lifetime. He is forty, so grew up in a time when racist, sexist and homophobic attitudes could not be openly expressed.

But what of his view of *naturally* civil England, a pre-PC civility that defines not only England, but Britain?

Yes, it is true that in the '40s, '50s and '60s, Brits were much more outwardly polite to each other, yet strangers in their midst were subjected to constant indignities, discrimination, insults and sometimes racist violence. Brazen notices declaring, 'No Blacks, No Irish, No Dogs', were everywhere. Females, too, were second-class citizens denied real respect, choices or equal opportunities. Working-class people knew their place and stayed put in it. The pyramid with a few at the top and everyone else below them was solid and unyielding. The structure depended on a belief system that things were the way they were because they were meant to be. Class determines the future for millions[12] and racism is respectable once again.[13]

The two world wars and the welfare state which was set up in the '50s, transformed Britain. In some ways. Deference gave way to more assertiveness, rights took

---

12 'The Labour Force Survey Reveals Class Discrimination in UK Workplaces', 13 November 2015: https://www.slatergordon.co.uk/media-centre/blog/2015/11/the-labour-force-survey-reveals-class-discrimination-in-uk-workplaces/

13 See, for example, Katie Forster, 'Hate crimes soared by 41% after Brexit vote, official figures reveal', *The Independent*, 13 October 2016: http://www.independent.co.uk/news/uk/crime/brexit-hate-crimes-racism-eu-referendum-vote-attacks-increase-police-figures-official-a7358866.html

over from predestination. The state took care of citizens from cradle to grave, trade unions became more powerful, Labour governments were voted in. However, this was not some bloodless revolution. (Revolutions are thought to be very un-British.) In the home and in society, inequality between men and women and the classes continued. The country remained stable and recognisable. (Under Apartheid, South Africa, too, was much more stable and secure than it has been since it became a democracy.) A stable society is often thought to be contained, conformist, intransient, weighed down by a sense of inevitability.

The '60s started to shake things up, but again, the claims made on behalf of this counter culture are much exaggerated, and so too the eventual impact. Yes, there was much free sex, love, drug taking, hippy happiness and rock 'n' roll. And briefly, in 1968, student revolts flared up across the West – although all of which were duly stamped out by state forces. But this decade and the '70s, too, continued to be racist and sexist and homophobic. By wearing bell-bottoms and flowers in one's hair, an illusion was created of a collapsing social order. It didn't happen. Thatcher and Reagan came into power at the fag end of this so-called social cataclysm. PC arrived soon after. It was a way of challenging the hold of the right and, more importantly, to create a more empathetic consciousness and modernism. Its aims were virtuous.

When Andre Gray, the Premier League footballer who, in 2012 and 2014, had sent out homophobic and racist tweets, he was relatively unknown. In 2017, these tweets came to light and Gray was properly castigated by the FA. He was fined and seemed to be genuinely sorry. After the public humiliation, he said, 'I am not the guy I was back then and will continue to work hard both on and off the pitch to become a better person.'[14]

To be a better person. To be a better nation. To be a better world. That is what PC is trying to do. And has, up to a point, done. Most young Britons get that. In these tempestuous and emotive times, I feel compelled to defend and rehabilitate socially responsible political correctness. Well, someone has to.

This book is divided into three parts.

In Part I, I go back to the origins and evolution of

---

14 MailOnline, August 2016.

political correctness to trace the history and development of the 'ideology' that first appeared in the US and was then imported into the UK.

Part II focuses on contemporary debates and cacophonies, including the myths, lies, follies and truths. Then the arguments for and against political correctness will be laid out and interrogated. At the end of this section I will examine current tensions and arguments between the new 'free speech' model army and their opponents. A critique of the negative effects of some aspects of modern political correctness will be included, so too the highly organised strikes against progressive individuals and institutions.

In Part III, I will go on to look at the cultural/social Darwinism that has engendered this age of political uncertainty and chaos, endorsed racisms, populism, sexual degradation and human rights breaches. The book will end with a rallying cry. Those of us who believe PC is a civilising mission must resist the reactionaries who want to preserve and reassert old ways and inherited advantages, worst of all, nail down social values for ever more.

Part I

The Road to Edification
or Perdition?

HERE BEFORE YOU is a smorgasbord of comments and opinions on PC. It is a small selection of choice examples from the early '90s to 2017. They provide a slide show of how wildly – and widely – people disagree about PC, its function and effects.

✻   ✻   ✻

'Watch What You Say: Thought Police'

COVER OF *NEWSWEEK*, DECEMBER 1990

'[PC] replaces old prejudices with new ones. It declares certain topics off-limits, certain expressions off-limits, even certain gestures off-limits. What began as a crusade for civility has soured into a cause of conflict and even censorship.'

PRESIDENT BUSH SR, SPEAKING AT
MICHIGAN UNIVERSITY, MAY 1991

'Changes to language, whether the introduction of American neologisms or attempts to reduce racism or sexism, have always got Disgusted of Tunbridge Wells hopping ... [Those who attack PC] aren't libertarians. Purportedly hating authoritarianism, it's the threatened loss of their own authority and supremacy they can't stand.'

ANNE KARPF, *THE GUARDIAN*, SEPTEMBER 1992

'This misnamed fashion for what people call "political correctness" amounts to testing everything, every aspect of life ... so that people feel intimidated and browbeaten ... Any questioning ... of the current fashions usually elicits a vitriolic response – whether it is a wish to teach people the basic principles of English grammar ... or suggesting that in certain circumstances it may be necessary and sensible to administer a smack to your child.'

PRINCE CHARLES, SPEECH TO THE NEWSPAPER SOCIETY,
LONDON, MAY 1994

'Can it really be true that the fabric of our nation is being undone not by poverty, unemployment and deprivation but a mere idea, a half-baked one at that? Apparently yes. The virus of political correctness is out to get all of us. And if it can't get to us, then it will get to our children ... the opposite of political correctness is not tolerance. Instead PC is being used to lunge at the heart of anyone who suggests there is something wrong with the status quo...'

SUZANNE MOORE, *THE GUARDIAN*, 1994

'PC is a dirty word in nineties Britain. To call someone PC is less a description than an insult, carrying with it accusations of everything from Stalinism/McCarthyism to (even worse?) having no sense of humour ... What PC has done is achieve the remarkable double whammy of offending both the right and a good deal of the left at the same time. In terms of the right, this alienation was inevitable. In terms of the left, however, ... it has been a more complex and tragic affair ... With the evils of nationalism and ethnic cleansing once again inside the borders of Europe, the idea of Britain as a genuinely multicultural society where all the voices are included and protected may sound like a liberal cliché but it could also become apolitical necessity.'

SARAH DUNANT, EDITOR, INTRODUCTION TO
THE WAR OF THE WORDS, VIRAGO PRESS, 1994

'The danger to intellectual life today comes not from political correctness but from those who elevate it to a threat. It's the old game of victim blaming: suddenly the real evil is not racism but anti-racism; the real villains are not oppressors but the oppressed. Although one expects nothing else from right wingers, intelligent liberals ought to know better. Instead, alas, many have meekly accepted the Right's mischievous terms of debate.'

FRANCIS WHEEN, *THE GUARDIAN*, JANUARY 1996

'Political Correctness has become an assault course for employers in a world where even a gift of a box of chocolates to a woman colleague can be misconstrued as sexual harassment and Irish jokes are under threat because the Commission for Racial Equality has identified Irish people living in the UK as an ethnic minority enduring unacceptable abuse.'

MAURICE CHITTENDEN, *SUNDAY TIMES*, JULY 1997

'Noddy and Sambo make a comeback ... *Ten Little Nigger Boys* comes in from the cold ... Bookshops and publishers are reporting an interest in 'incorrect' fiction as parents ... characters such as Golliwog and Big Ears are back in favour ... Little Black Sambo sells as fast as it is reproduced.'

CATHERINE ELLSWORTH, *SUNDAY TELEGRAPH*, JANUARY 1997

'Political correctness is the new cancer. It erodes rather than builds; divides rather than unites.'

'I am heartily sick of the PC brigade and all the claptrap they spout. I want my country to stay British and Christian and for all to see this. I want to see Union Jack flags, Christmas decorations, Easter eggs and English spoken as I walk down the street.'

'[From a British soldier:] Did I see my friends perish just so Tony's Cronies could give away our sovereignty to the PC brigade?'

COMMENTS POSTED BY MAILONLINE READERS IN NOVEMBER 2007

'The country is well nigh paralysed by political correctness.'

ANN WIDDECOMBE, *DAILY EXPRESS*, APRIL 2007

'The short lived experiment of multiculturalism has failed and the days of the general public meekly bowing to the forces of PC are over. The average voters, namely the vast majority unlike the ranks of the Labour party, broadcasting editing suites and union headquarters are sick and tired of this PC nonsense.'

BNP WEBSITE, APRIL 2007[15]

'The kind of people that say "political correctness gone mad" are usually using that phrase as a kind of covert action to attack minorities or people that they disagree with ... And I'm sick, I'm really sick – 84 per cent

---

15 This has now been removed from the website.

of you in this room that have agreed with this phrase, you're like those people who turn around and go, "You know who the most oppressed minorities in Britain are? White, middle-class men." You're a bunch of idiots.'

STEWART LEE, HERESY, BBC RADIO 4, MAY 2007

'HEALTH & SAFETY: PC's armed, militant wing, responsible for all that pettifogging, intrusive legislation that doesn't actually make anyone feel healthier or safer.'

JAMES DELINGPOLE, DAILY TELEGRAPH, MAY 2011

'It's now very common to hear people say "I'm rather offended by that…" Well, so fucking what?'

'So some fucking newspaper misquotes a humorous interview I gave, which itself misquoted me and now I'm the Antichrist. I give up.'

STEPHEN FRY, TWITTER, 2010
(HE THEN QUIT TWITTER FOR A WHILE)[16]

---

16 '@StephenFry quits Twitter… again?', The Media Blog, 1 November 2010: http://themediablog.typepad.com/the-media-blog/2010/11/stephen-fry-1005011110.html

'Political correctness is as severe a form of censorship as any.'

DUCHESS OF CORNWALL, LONDON PRESS AWARDS, MAY 2011

'We stated in an article on 26 September that Christmas has been renamed in various places Winterval.

Winterval was the collective name for a season of public events, both religious and secular, which took place in Birmingham in 1997 and 1998.

We are happy to make clear that Winterval did not replace Christmas.'

CORRECTION, *DAILY MAIL*, NOVEMBER 2011

'But who really thinks the right to offend is inalienable? Who believes that some hideous error was made when it became untenable to put a sign on the door of your pub saying: "No Irish, no blacks, no dogs"? Is there anyone who thinks the world would be a better place if high levels of homophobia were lauded as a wonderful sign that the right to free speech was being enthusiastically upheld? ... Free speech does not confer the right to be wrong, mistaken, biased or merely a doggedly axe-grinding pain-in-the-ass about your pet hates.'

DEBORAH ORR, *THE GUARDIAN*, SEPTEMBER 2012

'I could never appear on a discussion prog with @y_alibhai I would either end up with a brain haemorrhage or by punching her in the throat.'

'So just for the avoidance of any doubt: I am v sorry for tweet. It was wrong to joke abt punching + I completely withdraw and apologise.'

MICHAEL FABRICANT MP, TWITTER, JUNE 2014

'Political correctness is killing people.'

TED CRUZ, SPEAKING ON FOX NEWS DURING THE REPUBLICAN PRESIDENTIAL PRIMARY DEBATE, LAS VEGAS, DECEMBER 2015

'The big problem this country has is being politically correct.'

DONALD TRUMP, REPUBLICAN PRESIDENTIAL PRIMARY DEBATE, CLEVELAND, AUGUST 2015

'No I don't care. Show me pictures of coffins, show me bodies floating in water, play violins and show me skinny people looking sad. I still don't care.'

'Make no mistake, these migrants are like cockroaches.'

'I'd use gunships to stop migrants.'

COMMENTS MADE ON TWITTER AND ELSEWHERE
BY KATIE HOPKINS BETWEEN 2015 AND 2017

'Secretly everybody's getting tired of political correctness, kissing up. That's the kiss-ass generation we're in right now. We're really in a pussy generation. Everybody's walking on eggshells. We see people accusing people of being racist and all kinds of stuff. When I grew up, those things weren't called racist.'

CLINT EASTWOOD, *ESQUIRE*, AUGUST 2016

'Trump hit a vein. He hit the peak of political correctness, and he's an antidote to all that … And in a sense "you get what you deserve". That's democracy baby!'

RICKY GERVAIS, *HOLLYWOOD REPORTER*, MAY 2016

'The pendulum has swung very significantly the other way… If you are a white male, tough. You are an endangered species and you are going to have to work twice as hard.'

JOHN ALLAN, CHAIRMAN OF TESCO, MARCH 2017

'[The comment] was intended to be humorous, a bit hyperbolic.'

'I have been a committed advocate of greater diversity and very much regret if my remarks have given the opposite impression.'

JOHN ALLAN, IN RESPONSE TO CRITICISM OF HIS ABOVE COMMENT, *THE INDEPENDENT*, MARCH 2017

'An Englishman, a Frenchman and an American man walk into a bar and make whatever jokes they want because – haven't you heard? – political correctness is dead. Donald Trump and Brexit have sent it to its grave. You can say whatever you like now, offend whoever you like! Well not quite.

From the gender neutral ashes of political correctness

a new sort of PC culture has risen. You could call it populist correctness: a virulent policing of language and stifling of debate that is rapidly and perniciously insinuating itself into daily life in Trump's America and Brexit Britain.

Populist correctness is smearing and silencing of points of view by labelling them "elitist" – and therefore at odds with the will of the people and good of the country.'

ARWA MAHDAWI, THE GUARDIAN, FEBRUARY 2017

'At a time when this country is crying out for frank discussion on issues such as race and sexuality, debate is being closed down because those who find offence in every-thing [*sic*] cry "racist" or "sexist" … the recognition of diversity has grown into a cancerous cultural tyranny that blocks open debate.'

TREVOR PHILLIPS, DAILY MAIL, FEBRUARY 2017

'As academics with positions at UK universities, we wish to express our dismay at this attempt to silence campus discussions about Israel, including its violation of the rights of Palestinians for more than 50 years. It is with disbelief that we witness explicit political interference in university affairs in the interests of Israel under the thin disguise of concern about antisemitism.'

PROFESSOR JONATHAN ROSENHEAD, PROFESSOR MOSHÉ
MACHOVER AND 240 OTHERS, LETTERS PAGE,
THE GUARDIAN, FEBRUARY 2017

'"Pathetic, useless fat black piece of shit Abbott. Just a piece of pig shit pond slime who should be fucking hung (if they could find a tree big enough to take the fat bitch's weight)" ... Once, the pushback was against the actual arguments for equality and social justice. Now the pushback is the politics of personal destruction.'

DIANE ABBOTT WRITING ABOUT THE ABUSE AND THREATS
SHE RECEIVES, THE GUARDIAN, FEBRUARY 2017

'Just because they're offended doesn't make them right. It's part of reasoned debate. If they're upset by it, so be it ... I would say the one thing you can never joke about in the UK, is Hillsborough. It's a tragedy that has touched people in a very specific way and I cannot

imagine anyone ever coming up with a joke about that
… You can joke about religion and I do often. You can
joke about death, you can joke about murders, and you
can joke about disasters. If comedy has any purpose
it does help people cope with stuff and make it OK.'

JIMMY CARR, *DESERT ISLAND DISCS*, MARCH 2017

'[Political correctness] … another way of looking at it
was that it was just plain courtesy.'

LORRIE MOORE, *GUARDIAN MAGAZINE*, MAY 2018

'The return of theocracy having been seen off, the new
threat is to freedom of speech. But "free speech" is kind
of an Aunt Sally anyway. Free speech is everywhere, in
ways that most people will endorse, abridged both *de
facto* and *de jure*. It's abridged *de facto* by good manners
(which is what about 80 per cent of "political correctness" adds up to) and by a social consensus, policed
by the bounds of acceptability. If you say something
offensive, you may well suffer an influx of angry eggs;
turn up at a costume party blacked up or dressed as a

Wehrmacht officer and unless your host is Taki you can expect to cop some flak. But you won't go to jail.

And "free speech" is abridged *de jure* by legal sanctions on libel, false advertising, incitement to violence, and (in some countries and more controversially) blasphemy, "hate speech", Holocaust denial and so on. We can and should argue about the limits law places on public discourse — I favour the barest minimum — but we should recognise that is what we are doing, rather than invoking an imaginary, unproblematic ideal called "free speech".'

SAM LEITH, *THE SPECTATOR*, JULY 2018

❖   ❖   ❖

So from these statements, are we any clearer on what PC is? It often seems to mean whatever its enemies want it to mean. More ominously, it has become an unanswerable accusation, a careless slur or a gag with which to muzzle both views and people. That is why hardly anyone today claims to be PC. It would be social suicide. I do, but there is a price to pay and I duly pay it. The vocal anti-PC alliance which includes some parliamentarians, the right-wing press, the royals, aggressive libertarians, Voltairean intellectuals and some on the left too, are hell-bent on intimidating and silencing the PC voice. In the name of free speech. In July 2018, anti-Trump Londoners got permission to fly a huge balloon of the President as a big baby while he was on a visit to the country. Right-wing commentators wanted the balloon banned. Oh, the irony.

Way back in 1994, Sarah Dunant observed, '[apocalyptically] PC is hailed as a movement which, if allowed to run unchecked, will curtail free speech, deny common sense, threaten the foundations of family life and rewrite our national and literary histories until all notions of western values are denied'. She, a dispassionate witness, was herself concerned that 'the cacophony of voices demanding attention' was endangering cultural and social cohesion.

Well, things have only got worse in the years that have gone by. Forebodings of civilisational annihilation have intensified, warnings become more extravagant.

Two forces, working in tandem, have fanned the flames of fear. On 9/11, Islamicists began their ideological and real assaults on all those seen as enemies, including non-conformist Muslims. They are on an unending unholy war to impose a religious correctness, to crush believers who have multiple identities and loyalties, and who feel part of common humanity in all its diversities. The jihadis are unconsciously aided and abetted by influential Westerners who have also declared an unholy war against various 'enemies within' – migrants, Muslims, minorities, lefties, human rights and equality activists and the millions who do not wish to leave the EU. Our country has never been more splintered, bitter and angry. PC is easy to pick on, but the truth is that we are in the middle of the latest cultural wars.

Regiments ranged against PC include prelapsarians, post-Enlightenment crusaders, fractious nationalists, sad nostalgics and powerful people with vested interests in defending the status quo. For this coalition of the disgruntled, history is a continuum, arguments and conflicts are simple and binary – between cowboys and Indians, or the West and the rest. The underpinning assumption is that sane, respectable humans subscribe to fixed versions of the past and present. Received wisdom, as we know, runs deep – and rarely yields to awkward veracities. Most people opt for an easy life and do not question dominant views.

Britain, for example, has its own very strict PC tenets which predate the term 'PC'. Both Houses of Parliament have formally prescribed behaviours and language; protocol is unchallengeable and oh, the rules, the rules! Though a republican, I have met the Queen on a few occasions. I was given strict instructions on how many words I was allowed to utter, curtseys and all that. I said I would greet her with an Indian namaste, pressing hands together. Her minders objected. I did it anyway. So what shall we call these strictures? Historical correctness? Furthermore, libel laws, editorial guidelines and broadcasting regulations are all accepted without much protest.

Until the end of the twentieth century, Britons were raised to be terribly polite and to avoid controversies. When I first came to this country, one was expected to avoid all talk about religion and politics with dinner hosts or college colleagues. Imagine being in the UK in the messy and chaotic early '70s and holding back from talking about the government. But that was the expectation. It kept the peace. That was perhaps social correctness.

The British public is still mostly polite with shop assistants, colleagues, public service workers. (I, being raised in a much ruder, class- and race-divided society in Uganda, truly value these courtesies.) In the real world, do any of us speak as we wish all the time? Say, an overweight man is eating a fat bag of chips. I think: stupid guy. But I don't say it aloud. Or a mother with a wailing child is too busy reading *Vogue*. Do I tell her to control her kid? No way. Racial abuse and sexual harassment on trains, buses or streets does not pass unnoticed. Incidents are filmed and reported. The perpetrators experience collective opprobrium. There is still a strong sense of what one may and may not say in public. Long may that last.

Think too of the way the right has been 'managing' and controlling language for decades. Remember how 'collateral damage' was neatly injected into the vocabulary of war in the late '90s? It was to neutralise the horror over civilian deaths in Afghanistan and Iraq. 'Rendition', similarly, was used to cover up the depravity of torture by Western powers. Religious objectors to terminations say they are 'pro-life', an incredibly benign label for their strident, nasty, anti-abortion missions. Trump has mounted a vendetta against major US newspapers who oppose him because he hates what they say about him. One could even (mischievously) suggest that this extreme right-winger is actually very PC, because he feels the pain when critical comments are said or written about him.

British politics has always been inordinately PC. Poor Gordon Brown never recovered from his 'gaffe' when, in 2010, he described Gillian Duffy, a voter in Rochdale, as a 'bigoted woman' after she heckled him about immigration. It was meant to be a private comment after an interview he had done for Sky News, but his mike was still on. That was the end of Mr Brown. Duffy had the right to speak as she wished. But to oppose her views during those tempestuous days was well-nigh impossible. Those who thought that Mrs Duffy had expressed prejudices, self-censored themselves. As so often happens, freedom to speak was only available to the person who expressed anti-immigrant views. Brown could not argue his position. We have had to learn to submit to such media-made commotions. As one progressive Labour MP said to me recently, 'I bite my tongue so much it bleeds. Some of my constituents no longer hide their prejudices. And I, it seems, must go along with those or they will run off and sell their stories to *The Sun* or *Mail* and then we'll get one of those anti-PC gales.' Politicians have also been caught out when they used racist or sexist language. They are forced to abjectly apologise. In 2017, for example, Tory MP Anne Marie Morris was suspended by her party for using a racist term, and Labour's Emma Dent Coad was named and shamed after she called Shaun Bailey, a black Tory London assembly member, a 'token ghetto boy'. Anti-PC contingents do not rush to town squares to protect these martyrs to free speech.

The unthinking, lazy denunciation of political correctness does not bear up to scrutiny. If everyone has an absolute and sacrosanct right to speak as they wish, why then, do we get so many blazing controversies over words spoken by elected men and women, or peers, or celebrities, or famous sportsmen? The most vociferous opponents of PC do not campaign to bring back slurs such as 'nigger' or 'yid'. Even they can see that would be a retrograde step.

Deborah Cameron, the linguist, wrote in 1989,

> So far as I know, there has never been a time when people were content merely to speak their language and not in addition speak *about* it; there has never been a culture which did not believe that some ways of using words were functionally, aesthetically or morally preferable to others – though equally there has never been one that did not violently disagree about which these ways were.

So, these arguments have gone on through history. Yet naysayers claim that until pesky PC arrived, there was a happy consensus on political and personal speech in the UK and the US, and on social organisation and power too. Either they are ill informed, or they are being 'economical with the truth' (a PC term coined by Edmund

Burke, the ethical eighteenth-century conservative politician and philosopher)

'What do you guys want? Am I to throw out my Enid Blytons and Marilyn Monroe poster? Am I a racist and sexist old bugger?' asked an exasperated old history teacher at a Christmas party. 'Not for me to say,' I replied. He got cross. He wanted a confrontation. I didn't want to give him one. I am tired of these unnecessary rows, which are a bit like drunks needing a brawl in a pub. I now slip away from more reasonable arguments, too. How many times can you tell people that words and acts cannot be separated neatly, that sometimes words, as Coriolanus said, incapacitate humans more than blows? I don't mean words that incite illegal actions, such as shouting 'fire!' in a crowded theatre, or Rwandan broadcasters saying Tutsis were like cockroaches during the genocide. I mean words and images that the more powerful use to disparage less powerful humans and deny them dignity. My racist fellow citizens often enjoin me to fuck off back where I came from. They don't touch me or throw me on to a departing boat, but each time I hear or read the words, I lose a bit more of myself and sense of belonging, my confidence is shaken.

Language is but one part of the reformation we PC followers have been striving for. We want the culture to be expansive, to include people of all colours, men and women, the disadvantaged and the over-advantaged. We want to redefine excellence, to affirm diversity, to make institutions open and just. We are people of all races, ethnicities, classes, ages, regions, sexualities and political persuasions. (Cameron and Clegg got on because they were, in essence, instinctively PC: open, modern, non-sexist, married to wives at ease in the multifarious world.) However, in this decade, our opponents – a significant number of white middle-class men, black and Asian conformists, and now some women too – resolutely discredit these reasonable aims, and get overwrought if systems, structures, presumptions and knowledge are examined. All of that must be conserved for years, decades, centuries. Contestation is felt to be vindictive, or reverse discrimination, people see it as the end of the world as they know it. I believe these are 'pre-emptive measures' (to use the right-wing PC term) to disable change agents. All we want is a share. It's not a takeover – it is time.

I moved to Britain from Uganda in 1972. It wasn't easy to resettle and feel accepted, those were tough old days. But most of us incomers wanted to believe the country was gruff but fair and tolerant. Not so. The first time I became acutely aware of embedded, unrecognised, institutional discrimination was at my interview at Oxford when I was applying to do my MPhil in literature not long after I moved. I had a first-class degree from Makerere University, Uganda, an internationally rated institution. Seven white, male dons sat in front of me. They did not think I could 'fulfil the arduous requirements of the course'. When I said my favourite writers were V. S. Naipaul and Toni Morrison, only two of them knew the names.[17] One of the interviewers then sneered: 'If you want to do that sort of thing you should go to Leeds or somewhere like that.' I did get into Oxford and I showed them. But how many other 'outsiders' with aspirations were discouraged or kept out?

---

17 Both of these great authors went on to win Nobel prizes for literature.

Something had to be done to shake up European and American complacencies and knowledge monopolies.

The same is true of my industry: the media, which is still almost entirely white, Oxbridge and middle class. Most British journalists and editors do not share or properly understand the experiences and lives of millions in the UK, or indeed, three quarters of the world. This clearly has serious consequences. They cannot report on global matters as well as they should because they are detached as well as conceited. Exceptional professionals who break out of these walls of complacency include, among others, Lyse Doucet, Jeremy Bowen, Robert Fisk, Christina Lamb, Owen Jones, Zoe Williams, Ian Birrell and Patrick Cockburn. Their reports and viewpoints do not reinforce set views and stereotypes. You would not get from them, for example, coarse commentaries based on notions of the 'civilised' West and 'uncivilised' rest. They do not look at the world through the scratched lenses of European imperialism.

Robert Mugabe's forced resignation, for example, was given much time and space in the British media, partly because this is not just any African country, but a homeland to old white settlers. They're kith and kin, I understand that. But the momentous story needed to be told in full. True, Mugabe became tyrannical, encouraged the victimisation of white farmers, and wrecked the economy. But earlier on in his life, he was imprisoned for a decade by colonial powers, humiliated and ill-treated, to the extent that he was not allowed to go to the funeral of his baby boy. He was imprisoned because he, like Mandela, wanted freedom and justice for his people. In what was Rhodesia, the most fertile land was stolen from black farmers by white rulers. When Zimbabwe became independent, the British government agreed to fund the buyback of that land, a promise never fully kept. Not one report took us back to that unresolved dispute. The impression was given that 'savage' blacks persecuted whites (many of whom still believe in their own supremacy) and that this persecution led to economic devastation. John Humphrys said so on the *Today* programme, so it is taken as factually impeccable. This is not fake news. It is half-news, which impedes proper understanding. A politically correct version would have been more complete and honest.

A Brief History of Political Correctness

So when exactly did the terms 'politically correct' and 'politically incorrect' enter the lexicon? And what happened next? There were a few embryonic and inchoate versions of 'political correctness' through the early part of the twentieth century. They came and went without making much impact. But the right was vigilant, alert and ready to repel half-formed challenges from their imagined enemies.

Opponents of PC believe the rot began with the Frankfurt School of philosophy founded in 1923, which included some German philosophers arguing for 'cultural Marxism', a combative socialist – and at times, thoroughly anti-American – credo. In its first incarnation, PC, it is thought, was an in-joke between ardent anti-capitalists in the 1930s. As they set about trying to remake the world, they seemed aware of their own occasional daftness. One of the typical gags went: 'Comrade, your statement is factually incorrect.' Reply: 'Yes, but it is politically correct.' (Trumpspeak is, when you think about it, often factually incorrect but politically correct. He who hates PC has mastered the art of PC better than old commies ever could.)

In Vladimir Nabokov's 1947 novel, *Bend Sinister*, you get a version of political correctness meaning group think. The Russian novelist was an individualist and free expression proponent. His beautifully written, un-PC novel *Lolita,* about an older man's sexual obsession with a twelve-year-old girl, is still controversial.

> A person who has never belonged to a Masonic Lodge or to a fraternity, club, union, or the like, is an abnormal and dangerous person ... It is better for a man to have belonged to a politically incorrect organization than not to have belonged to any organization at all.

Chairman Mao's Little Red Book seemed to confirm the worst fears of right-wingers and centrists, too. The compilations of quotes by Chairman Mao were published between 1964 and 1976. For millions of Americans anyone who asks for speech restraint is channelling communist villains such as Mao, Stalin, Castro et al. You can understand why. These dictatorial men habitually issued severe injunctions on the correct way to be political and patriotic.

The USA

The Second World War ended in 1945 and the Cold War started in 1947. Paranoid patriotism intensified and inevitably led to McCarthyism, which used the language of freedom to push a right-wing fundamentalism in order to control words and actions and check thoughts and motives. Essentially, you were a communist unless you could prove otherwise. Hundreds of Americans had their lives destroyed. Oppressive conformity almost always leads to declared or undeclared rebellions. The American left was wounded but morally strengthened,[18] and the civil rights movement located itself in this politics of fairness and equality.

In the '60s and '70s lefties used the term PC, often among themselves, to mock each other or for a laugh, sometimes, to curtail excessively dogmatic positioning. It only became a concern when it was no longer a big joke. American stability and security depends on keeping its self-image and myths sacrosanct.

Black American female writers in the '70s, struggling

---

18 See Mari Jo Buhle, Paul Buhle and Dan Georgakas, *Encyclopaedia of the American Left*, 2nd edn (Oxford: Oxford University Press, 1998).

then, as now, with double discrimination and double marginalisation, began to challenge language as well as received wisdom, mostly in a non-confrontational way. Toni Cade Bambara, one of the first and most profound of these writers, for example, wrote in *The Black Woman: An Anthology*: 'A man cannot be politically correct and a chauvinist, too.' In this decade, PC, though a fringe issue, was often a disputed one between, say free love activists and anti-porn feminists. Students got into these skirmishes, but only half seriously.

PC then started to edge into mainstream America, mainly on campuses – the laboratories which create US leaders and power merchants. At first it was seen as a nuisance or just student silliness, par for the course. But the academic and political establishments started to notice and got a bit jumpy; these youngsters were not just being annoying, but potentially subversive. It was a response to political stasis. This was, as Sarah Dunant puts it:

> With America in the grip of a sustained period of right-wing government, preaching aggressive free market

economics and reduced government welfare, issues of race and gender, [issues always associated with the left] had been knocked off the political agenda. PC, both on and off campus, has helped to put them back on.[19]

The first heated disputes were not about language but the closed cannons at universities. Students and rebellious academic staff wanted to shake up the curriculum and interrogate the idea that excellence was an objective term and a judgement.

Dark forces were at work too, unconnected to PC. Evidence shows that from the '60s, right-wing American millionaires had been hyperactive, setting up think tanks and institutes, funding media training and providing endowments for conservative-leaning students and academic staff. Among some of the most secretive and effective were the Koch brothers and Richard Mellon Scaife. Fanatic economic and social Darwinians, they abominated welfare, state healthcare provision, civil rights and the 'liberal academy'. According to

---

19 Sarah Dunant, *The War of the Words: The Political Correctness Debate* (Virago Press, 1994), p. ix.

Jane Mayer, author of a recent extraordinary exposé of organised libertarianism and extreme capitalism in the USA, such backers sponsored, and continue to sponsor, what seems to me, purposeful and well-organised *conceptual correctness*.[20] One has to ask why these programmes have never been seen as a threat to pluralist democracy, which they certainly continue to be in our current times.

In the mid-1980s, US exceptionalism, patriotic imperatives, propaganda and a sense of predestination were questioned by many of the country's own citizens. The greatest nation on earth, blessed by God, felt the ground tremble a little. Feminists, gays and anti-racists were demanding a more inclusive curriculum, respect, dignity and real equality. They pushed in from the periphery, edged towards the centre. Language was examined and challenged, so too the canon, first-world hubris and domination, and, most audacious of all, power. The establishment found it all intolerable. Some academics got anxious; others defensive. Many had thrown

---

20 *Scribe*, 2016, See chapters 1, 2 and 3. See also Mayer's essay in *New York Times*, 30 June 2010.

themselves into anti-colonialist political and cultural liberationist movements when young and green and easily roused, but that was the distant past. Wasn't growing up, in part, adapting to established conventions and norms? Only nuisances such as Noam Chomsky and Henry Louis Gates Jr carried on and on, berating their own nation. By then, those same ever-vigilant, billionaire families decided to 'protect' and promote ultraconservatism in the USA. They remain hyperactive.[21]

It did not take long for the media and politicians to join this crusade.

Opponents of PC project themselves as impassioned, noble upholders of freedom of speech. Freedom of speech is a precious ideal for all of us who promote PC too. But we are not absolutists. Citizens are not at liberty to say whatever they damn well want, not even in the US, which has the First Amendment, a constitutional guarantee of freedom of expression. Here are but two examples: during the First World War, Charles T. Schenck, a member of the Socialist Party of America, published anti-war leaflets and

---

21 Mayer, op. cit. See also Carole Cadwalladr's investigations in *The Observer* in 2017 and 2018.

passed them to drafted soldiers. He was arrested, tried and convicted. He appealed to the Supreme Court, argued that the conviction violated his First Amendment rights. He lost the case. Justice Oliver Wendell Holmes Jr declaimed,

> restrictions on free speech are permissible during times of war ... The most stringent protection of free speech would not protect a man in falsely shouting 'fire' in a crowded theatre and causing a panic ... The question in every case is whether the words used in such circumstances are of such a nature as to create a clear and present danger that they will bring about the substantive evils that Congress has a right to prevent.

So, there you have it. Ordinary citizens, it turned out, were not free to argue peacefully against the state's decision to go to war. (This ruling was so embedded in American consciousness, it prevented many from objecting to the wars in Vietnam and Iraq.) In 2006, Tony Judt, the globally respected American public intellectual, was suddenly informed that he no longer had a venue booked in which he was to talk on Israel and US foreign policy. Excuses were given but Judt's supporters suspected the subject was felt to be too controversial by the owners.[22] In 2006, Judt invited me to New York to deliver talks on the Iraq War and discrimination faced by Western Muslims. He also had to cancel these and explained that he had been advised that I was putting myself in danger with the authorities. A number of blameless Muslims had been arrested at the time. You see? Free speech was not an unconditional right for this outspoken journalist. An African-American lecturer I knew was hounded after he was 'caught' speaking passionately at a student rally on white cultural hegemonies. This ensured that he was unable to obtain another university job, and he had to requalify as a social worker. Between 1998 and 2015 the award-winning British documentary maker, Nick Broomfield, could not get his film on Kurt Cobain shown on any US TV channel. The usually edgy Sundance Film Festival refused to screen it. Vested interests were being protected.[23] Organisations and individuals who always stand

---

22 See *New York Review of Books*, 16 November 2006.

23 See 'Endless Love', by Daphne Merkin, *New Yorker*, 8 June 1998.

up for free expression sucked it up. Freedom was available to some: the approved, the obliging. What kind of freedom is that? The more I think about and examine these questions, the more I see the various hypocrisies, lies and double standards of free expression champions. As far as I know, every one of them has kept silent on the divisive issue of whether all criticism of Israel is anti-Semitic, a slur now common in the public space. In the summer of 2018, several prominent journalists – among them Nick Cohen of *The Observer* – accused the BBC, in a devastating critique, of failing to cover the allegedly deeply unwholesome tactics of the Leave campaign before and since the referendum. Mounting evidence seems to make no difference. In effect, the BBC is 'censoring' truths because the vote was won by Brexiters, because it is nervous about challenging the now embedded narrative about the 'will of the people'. Read it and weep.[24]

In a compelling essay, the American writer Moira Weigel described the real aims and objectives of political

---

24 Nick Cohen, 'What is the Point of the BBC if it is Frightened of Journalism? *New European*, 19 July 2018.

correctness and also the systematic, well-resourced counter-offensives:

> many universities were creating new 'studies departments', which interrogated the experiences of and emphasised the cultural contributions of groups that had previously been excluded from the academy and from the canon: queer people, people of colour and women. This was not so strange. These departments reflected new social realities. The demographics of college students were changing, because the demographics of the United States were changing.[25]

In 1987, Chicago professor Allan Bloom wrote a bestselling book, *The Closing of the American Mind*, in which he argued that multiculturalism was corrupting the integrity and sapping the vigour out of university life. It was a seminal but seriously flawed publication, because Bloom's own mind was too closed to see that his was, in effect, a manifesto for conformity and permitted dissent.

---

25 Moira Weigel, 'Political Correctness: How the Right Invented a Phantom Enemy', *The Guardian*, 30 November 2016.

For Bloom, intellectual debate had to be conducted within set norms; cannons were sacred as were ways of thinking. He seemed most exercised about African-American students at Cornell University. They were too 'militant' because they demanded an African Studies department. Wanting to study James Baldwin, Maya Angelou, Toni Morrison, Derek Walcott or Chinua Achebe was, apparently, tantamount to sedition.

Dinesh D'Souza, right-wing and brash, wrote his own scornful – at times, unproven – account of what was going badly wrong on American campuses. These protectionist, biased polemicists were glorified as freethinkers. Their cause and case has never properly been examined. Canons are not tablets of stone. They change. They always have. Bloom and D'Souza simply wanted to keep the club exclusive, to keep out upstarts. I once publicly debated with D'Souza. He exhorted the audience to believe in his maniacal conspiracy theories about left-wing plots to take over America. McCarthy himself would have been proud to know such a patriot. In 2017, when neo-Nazis marched in Charlottesville to provoke a race war, Trump refused to condemn them and was, in turn, defended by

D'Souza. Age has not mellowed these uber-conservatives who have cloaked backers in high places.[26]

In 1989 came the fall of the Berlin wall. When Margaret Thatcher left office in 1990, communism was on its way down and out. Occidental capitalist consumerism had seemingly totally trounced all other political and economic ideologies.[27] There was no other way. Lattes and handbags were going to unite and gratify the planet. Except it didn't all quite work out that way. Just as the US claimed victory and vindication, a good number of its own citizens were refusing hand-me-down values. Chauvinists were not impressed. Grumblings and counterclaims? Fervid rejection of the good life? The Cold War was over, and another had begun despite the ingrates and subversives. The US always needs to define itself through its enemies, outsiders and insiders – real and imagined.

In 1990, *New York Times* reporter Richard Bernstein,

---

26 Both received money from the F. W. Olin family foundation. The Olins, like the Koch brothers and Scaife, targeted liberal institutions and equality measures. See Mayer, op. cit.

27 See, for example, the triumphalist books by Francis Fukuyama and Niall Ferguson, both of whom keenly believe that the West has won resoundingly and for ever.

published an agitated article entitled 'IDEAS & TRENDS; The Rising Hegemony of the Politically Correct'. Revisionist disciples of 'Stalinist Orthodoxy' were accused of closing off debate, forcing people to conform. I beg your pardon? This was the acme of Reaganism; the country was marching rightwards. Republicans controlled money, messages, policies, politics, arms and trade – even the future itself. How could a minority of resisters ever storm such an impenetrable wall? All they could do was paint graffiti on it.

Bernstein was most alarmed that in universities such as Berkeley, certain opinions about race equality, ecology, feminism and foreign policy had taken root. Did he really think equality and human rights were simply points of view? How far would he have taken this dangerous absurdity? Should American universities assiduously teach both the arguments for and against slavery and the Holocaust? In the twenty-first century, it is still impossibly difficult higher education establishments in the US that teach students about the ideals underpinning socialism and communism or Israel's disregard for international laws.

Other 'respectable' newspapers and universities joined the fray. (So now we know. Panic trending happened long before the internet arrived.) According to Weigel,

> the phrase 'politically correct' rarely appeared before 1990. That year, it turned up more than 700 times. In 1991, there were more than 2,500 instances. In 1992, it appeared more than 2,800 times. Like Indiana Jones movies, these pieces called up enemies from a melange of old wars: they compared the 'thought police' spreading terror on campuses to fascists, Stalinists, McCarthyites, 'Hitler Youth', Christian Fundamentalists, Maoists and Marxists.[28]

One incident illustrated the dramatic, escalating clashes. In 1991, Harvard professor Stephan Thernstrom read from the diaries of slavers in his class. He was criticised in a student mag for 'racial insensitivity'. That was all. A journalist, John Taylor, blew this up alarmingly in the *New York Magazine*, claiming the academic

---

28 Weigel, *The Guardian*, op. cit.

had been pitilessly hounded: '"Racist!" "Racist!" "The man is a racist!" Such denunciations, hissed in tones of self-righteousness and contempt, vicious and vengeful, furious, smoking with hatred – such denunciations haunted Stephan Thernstrom for weeks ... It was hellish, this persecution. Thernstrom couldn't sleep. His nerves were frayed, his temper raw.'[29]

These were gross exaggerations, bordering on lies. In an interview later, Thernstrom denied that he had been targeted and harassed. Such ostracisation never took place. One of the students who criticised the professor later explained that they had simply pointed out inaccuracies in his lecture. 'To me, it's a big overreaction for him to decide not to teach the course again because of that,' she said. Martin Kilson, professor of government at Harvard, concluded that 'there is no Thernstrom case'. Kilson called the episode a 'marvellous example of the skill of the neocons at taking small events and translating them into weapons against the pluralistic thrust on American campuses'.[30]

---

29 *New York Magazine*, 21 January 1991.

30 Jon Wiener, *Historians in Trouble: Plagiarism, Fraud, and Politics in the Ivory Tower* (New Press, 2005), pp. 68–69.

Many of these articles recycled the same stories of campus controversies from a handful of elite universities, often exaggerated or stripped of context. Lies were circulated. Right-wingers and establishment-keepers have disfigured language, fabricated evidence to get public support for unjustified wars, framed innocent people, excluded those on the left from jobs and opportunities – all in the national interest, of course. In 1985, *The Observer* published a story about how MI5 secretly vetted BBC appointments. The brilliant children's writer Michael Rosen, a graduate trainee in 1972, was dismissed because he was on the left, and because he had worked on a project which had clips of US soldiers being tested with LSD.[31]

In 1991, George Bush Sr lambasted PC and accused its proponents of stealing American liberties and rights.[32] (And yet his own son, when President, insisted that the US–UK alliance responsible for the murdering of

---

31 David Leigh and Paul Lashmar, 'The Blacklist in Room 105', *The Observer*, 18 August 1985.

32 George Bush speech, 'Remarks at the University of Michigan Commencement Ceremony in Ann Arbor', 4 May 1991: http://www.presidency.ucsb. edu/ws/?pid=19546

civilians in Iraq had to be described as 'collateral damage'.) In our times, the planned withdrawal of welfare support for the needy is described as 'austerity measures'. The aim must be to evoke the sacrifices willingly made by people during the Blitz.

Those who have declared war on PC do not listen to counter arguments or reason. All hang onto hand-me-down credos and traditions, knowledge and assumptions, imagining that sinister plotters are everywhere trying to bring down their civilisations and nations.

Bernstein carried on his emotive vendetta. In 1995, he wrote a book, *Dictatorship of Virtue*, accusing multiculturalists of being like the mobs in the Reign of Terror in France. Here's a taste:

> Hiding behind the innocuous, unobjectionable, entirely praiseworthy goal of eliminating prejudice from the human heart lies a certain ideology, a control of language, a vision of America that, presented as consensual common sense, is actually highly debatable. By its very nature it thrusts the concepts of 'racism' and 'sexism' and the various other isms to the forefront, turning them

from ugly aberrations into the central elements of American life and implicitly branding anyone who does not share that assumption to be guilty of the very isms that he feels do not lie in his heart.

Too much of the text is like this, hyperbolic and paranoid. I felt sorry for him by the end. But also impatient. It seems to me that white power relinquishes nothing. So long secure and proud, it is determined to define and control the forces now ranged against that power, including cultural protests and desires.

Those against political correctness, like cowboys, circled the wagons, metaphorically armed and fortified themselves. Millions more have joined the defensive and aggressive enclosures.

The UK

PC as we know it now, reached the UK in the mid-1980s. The special relationship means that what happens in the US soon blows over to this country. In both countries the right was holding on tightly, ruthlessly to power.

Culture and society became contested sites. I am proud to say I was part of that resistance in both countries. In 1986, I was invited to join a prestigious US–UK network which met every year alternating between Britain and America. The predominantly white club reinforced the theologies of Thatcher and Reagan. Unbelievers and outsiders like me were pitted against politicians, generals, public intellectuals and journalists who were committed to the two leaders. Debates and discussions were often heated, right-wing delegates were rattled by our challenges. I once sat next to a rabid neocon who accused me of being an anti-American infiltrator and Jew-hater. The encounters were testing but necessary.

In some ways it felt like the third significant liberation struggle of my life. The first was when I objected to and campaigned against colonialism and South African apartheid while growing up in Uganda. Subjugators and their descendants can never really understand how we felt, or why we will not accept their glorified versions of an exploitative history. Everything I know about power and egalitarianism was learnt when I was but an overemotional child, with an overdeveloped sense of injustice. Adulthood enabled me to articulate those values and emotions.

In 1972, I found myself in Britain, an exile who had to fight against racism and for fundamental rights and dignity. I felt fortunate to be living in a secure and relatively free country, and still do, but could not tolerate its class pyramid and embedded race hierarchy. Perhaps, inevitably, I became a ferocious equality warrior. There were many memorable clashes over those early years when racism was in your face and frightening. In 1980, I joined a demonstration against a march organised by the National Front in south London. The Met, at the time, had many NF sympathisers. I was racially abused by one of the police officers, whose job was to protect the public. He tripped me over. The resulting gash on my knee was my badge of honour. I still have a scar.

But I digress. As the Thatcher–Reagan free market and nationalistic mission became entrenched, guerrilla opposition to it mounted, first in the US, then here. The forces of conservatism seemed inexorable.

This is when and why Ken Livingstone turned the Greater London Council (GLC) into a raucous, blazing tower of political correctness. Other Labour councils followed suit. They saw themselves as heroic, anti-Thatcherite insurgents. I worked then as a senior lecturer at the Southwark Adult Education Institute, run by the Inner London Education Authority. Both the GLC and ILEA were attacked daily by right-wing tabloids.

The popular culture, daily discourse, political environment and institutional behaviours reinforced white rights and might. Non-Europeans were belittled, scorned, excluded and brutalised, sometimes for a laugh, mostly to keep us in their place. My mother was thrown off a bus near Shepherd's Bush roundabout; the driver shouted that she smelled like a 'curry shop'. White passengers sniggered. The driver maybe thought he was Alf Garnett, that frightfully popular xenophobe in *Till Death Do Us Part*.

According to journalist Sean O'Grady:

By the 1980s [PC] had become a rallying point for those who wanted to liberate academia from the Dwems – dead white European males – such as Shakespeare or

Chaucer, and to open up the literary canon to minority groups ... In the 1970s in the US and the 1980s in Britain it did a lot of good, especially in rooting out the casual, popular racist language many indulged in without thinking or, indeed, necessarily meaning offence ... Anyone who remembers the easy and offensive racial stereotyping in British TV shows such as *Love Thy Neighbour* and *Mind Your Language* should see that the passage of 'nigger', 'wog' and 'Paki' into disuse (even if, occasionally reclaimed by some radicals), is political correctness at its best. Many would also now wince at the memory of Bernard Manning, Jim Davidson's comic West Indian character 'Chalky White', the Black and White Minstrel Show, the golliwog on Robertson's jam, and jokes about thick paddies. And if women who work for airlines would rather be called flight attendants than air hostesses or trolly dollies, that, again, is something we now easily and calmly accept.[33]

But that struggle is not quite over. And never calm.

---

33 *The Independent*, 26 September 2002.

Libertarians across the political spectrum began to get restive and resentful. Freedom of expression apparently did not include the right to freely oppose the idea of untrammelled freedom of expression. Their stance was often hypocritical, deceitful and at times, senseless.

Everyone in the West accepts curtailments to individual liberties. As I wrote earlier, communication is affected by libel laws, editors' style guides, the political climate, an understanding of decency, the watershed, broadcast and newspaper regulations, political, diplomatic and business conventions – the unwritten rules that guide public discourse. I have been stopped from writing what I wanted – none of it salacious or libellous – by lawyers who worked at *The Independent* where I was a columnist for eighteen years, and also by editors on other papers, who thought my views would not go down well with more conservative readers. Or because they feared vexatious legal actions.

The people who resisted PC have never objected to any of the above. But to point that out is to invite a gale of invective. They will, it seems, tolerate state and societal control over their words and ideas, but will not surrender to a progressive movement which critically examines values, behaviours, language and knowledge.

Right from the start, PC in this country was a small, stubborn agitation against rigid conventions, the way things are done and have always been done, and yes, the political takeover by the right in the UK and US. You can see why these challenges were not well received. You can see too why, just as with other historic rebellions, it had to be quashed. Our antecedents are the nineteenth-century radicals – Mary Wollstonecraft, agitators such as John Wilkes and the black British intellectual William Davidson who were inspired by Thomas Paine's *Rights of Man* and the suffragettes. They were seen as treasonous. As are we.

PC radicals refused to accept establishment verities and took on the privileged, who ran everything and believed they owned political and economic systems and information, as well as interpretations. Who decreed that a certain race, class and gender should be in charge in perpetuity? Well white middle-class men did, *obviously*. And some obliging ladies, too. And, it has to be said, some entryist black and Asian Britons.

Influential British traditionalists (some of whom still

love their golliwogs) set about demolishing political correctness, often by misrepresenting it and sometimes by fabricating information. Britons were told that Hackney Council had banned the words 'manhole covers' because the term was sexist, Islington had banned 'Baa Baa Black Sheep' and that Brent Council was sending disruptive black kids on fully paid holidays to Cuba – just three examples among very many more.

In 1987, Labour MP Clive Soley raised the problem of press misrepresentations in the Commons:

> I recommend to hon. Members the University of London Goldsmith's College interim report entitled 'Media Coverage of London Councils'. It focused on a series of bizarre stories about the activities of local authorities in London and it stated: 'We investigated the background to these stories and spoke wherever possible to the journalists who wrote them. Our conclusion is that not one of these stories is accurate. A few appear to have been conjured out of thin air; the rest, although loosely connected with some basis of fact, have got important details wrong and are misleading.'

I summarise the rest of Soley's stirring speech.[34]

The MP gave examples from the report of how many false stories were picked up and snowballed. The Hackney Council 'manhole' story first appeared in the *London Standard* of 27 February 1986. Attributed to a *Standard* reporter, who claimed the council had banned the term. Other tabloids soon picked up the unsubstantiated claims. *The Sun*'s headline screamed, 'NOW MANHOLE IS A DIRTY WORD'. Councillors were mocked, called 'loony'. Keith Waterhouse wrote a column in the *Daily Mirror*, recycled the myths and untruths and describing the council members as 'barking mad' and a 'gang of lunatics'. Local newspapers picked up these tales of 'lunacy' and they went viral before the age of the internet. Facts didn't matter. Hackney Council had never issued any instruction, memo or report about the use of the word 'manhole'.

Chester Stern claimed in the *Mail on Sunday* that black bin liners had been banned at Bernie Grant's 'left-wing Haringey Council' because they were 'racially

---

34 Hansard, 27 November 1987.

offensive'. The report was made up. Corrections, if made, came long after the damage was done and were placed in inconspicuous spots on inside pages.

Around this time, journalist David Jones of *The Sun* published a scoop.[35] The London Borough of Brent, he claimed, was providing cash to anti-social black youths to visit Cuba. The story was false. The council did not fund such trips. It was a youth service initiative with money raised locally from the public. There was no preferential treatment of blacks. People were quoted who could not be found, and David Jones refused to comment (other than maintaining that he did speak to all those he quoted). The story was repeated (anonymously) in the *Daily Mail*. After that, according to Caribbean Exchange, which ran the project, it became much more difficult to raise money and worse, it sowed racial disharmony.

Soley pointed out such virulent journalism was a new phenomenon:

---

35 David Jones, 'Freebie Trip for Blacks but White Kids Must Pay. Barmy Brent Does it Again!', *The Sun*, 26 February 1987.

One of the saddest aspects about the debate is that in the last century and earlier this century newspapers would have protected minority groups and run impressive campaigns to protect minority rights. That practice has been undermined and destroyed in recent years by some newspapers. It is also significant that these reports occurred in the run-up to a general election.

He gave this example: on 25 May 1986 the *Mail on Sunday*'s Liz Lightfoot ran a piece under the headline 'BERNIE'S BANTER IS BAFFLING'. The article claimed that 'Bernie Grant, controversial leader of Haringey Council, has caused uproar over a scheme to teach West Indian dialect in the borough's schools.' The story, a calculated mix of fact and fiction, was picked up by a number of other papers. *The Sun*'s piece on the matter referred to the latest craze of London's Haringey Council which

wants children to be taught West Indian dialect Creole … they will be understood in the backstreets of Kingston, Jamaica, and probably nowhere else in the world … But don't imagine that Bernie's antics will afflict only one suffering part of London. Remember he is a Parliamentary candidate for Labour at the next Election … Labour is now the official barmy party.

When contacted, Miss Lightfoot protested that her report had been cut, and so may have got slightly hazy in its final form, or whatever. Some of what was published was unevidenced and aimed to incite passions rather than raise genuine awareness.

Most Britons refuse to accept that they are manipulated by sections of the media and gulled into believing lies and, more sinisterly, nudged towards holding prejudiced views of various citizens and communities. They really want to believe Britain has the greatest, liveliest and most honest newspapers and broadcast channels in the world, and that we should be proud of this sector.

By this time, resistance to perfectly reasonable political correctness had become a national obsession. White people, on the left and right, made common cause. They could not tolerate those who opposed or deconstructed their certainties, their shared sense of what it was to be

British. Beneath their differences there was a stronger bond than many of us challengers realised.

In the mid-1980s, alerts were issued by some British detractors, including the late Simon Hoggart[36] and the *Daily Mail*'s Ann Leslie, odd bedfellows. Leslie warned, 'They terrorise America and now they have established a beachhead on our shores.'[37] Melanie Phillips, railed against the 'plague'. Bryan Appleyard was withering:

> The new McCarthyism of Political Correctness is raging unabated ... in admittedly far-left Massachusetts, car bumpers are now plastered with a range of slogans to signal how slavishly the driver has bought the package. He/she is pro-choice (i.e. abortion), pro-recycling, anti-Bush and so on and so on. Use the word 'girl' over cocktails and you are as likely to be thrown out as if you had just said 'nigger'.[38]

Many of us felt excluded, misunderstood and somewhat

---

36 See *The Observer*, 11 July 1993.

37 *Daily Mail*, 14 September 1992.

38 *The Times*, 2 September 1992.

baffled too. Hadn't we been taught that in post-Enlightenment societies, ideas were contested through civil debate and argument? That change needed dissenters? That in a democracy all citizens were equal and at liberty to express thoughts and struggle for their ideals? Those foundational myths now felt like worthless avowals. It turned out there were severe limitations placed on those who questioned cultural, economic and political orthodoxies. Freedom was conformity. Breakouts of minor revolts were briefly thrilling and never a real threat to the natural order. Like punk rock or mini-skirts, or dope or Stuckists, they come and go. The centre always holds.

I bet most Brits have no idea about the censorship and self-censorship that operates secretly in all walks of life. When they were alive, the gin-sodden Queen Mother and dissipated Princess Margaret – am I allowed to write that? – were well protected from scrutiny. In 1967, 'almost the entire print-run of a Penguin book was burnt on the grounds that its contents were blasphemous and would be deeply offensive to many Christians'. The book was acclaimed French cartoonist Siné's *Massacre*.

The arsonist was none other than the prominent Penguin publisher Allen Lane.[39]

I have been thinking about all this for a very long time. I grew up unfree under British rule and then the various post-independence regimes of Uganda. I was only able to speak without fear in my twenties, living in the UK. The gift was precious and I never take it for granted. However, I have never been persuaded that extreme libertarianism is an unquestionably good thing for an individual or society. Many of Voltaire's declarations sound, to me, like fatuous rhetoric. 'Fight to the death' for those who express hateful views? How many such martyrs can you name? In 2011, I wrote,

A protracted and violent struggle against mental tyranny was fought by Europeans and … in the Arab lands citizens are inspired by the same emancipatory, human impulses. However, Voltaire's spiritual children can be fundamentalist, thoughtless and irrational, blind and deaf, unresponsive to the complexities of modern

---

39 Richard Webster, *A Brief History of Blasphemy: Liberalism, Censorship and the Satanic Verses* (Orwell Press, 1990), pp. 26–7.

life, of individual and group psychology, inequality and power.[40]

Artists and writers – among them Fay Weldon and Ian McEwan – were mightily offended when a copy of *The Satanic Verses* was burnt in Bradford.[41] Some of the most powerful and poetic writing poured out of their pens in defence of the writer's right to write. Nothing so noble poured out of any of them when Christian fundamentalists in the USA burnt copies of the Koran, a sacred text for millions. The god of fiction was more precious than the one god of a global monotheistic faith. It appears some books can be burnt without upsetting liberal sensibilities.

In 1984, Salman Rushdie wrote, 'Works of art, even works of entertainment, do not come into being in a social and political vacuum ... the way they operate in

---

40 *The Independent*, 11 April 2011.

41 This book is concerned with what happened in Britain. The fatwa against Rushdie was issued by Iranian leaders and was abhorred by most Britons, including Muslims.

a society cannot be separated from politics, from history. For every text, a context'.[42]

Unfortunately, those wise and instructive words, written in 1984, disappeared in the bonfire of vanities that followed the publication of *The Satanic Verses*, the most controversial novel ever written in post-war Britain. Mr Rushdie turned into a fundamentalist on free speech. The rest, as they say, is history.

---

42 'Outside the Whale', *Granta*, 1 March 1984.

Part II

The Arguments, Agendas,
Follies and Fakery

I N THIS PART, I critically review and summarise the arguments for and against political correctness from the 1980s to now. In the twenty-first century, the issue is proving to be both more disruptive and more meaningful than ever before. The two tribes are lined up; neither side acknowledges its own weaknesses or flawed judgements. I am a fully paid-up member of the PC taskforce but feel a certain responsibility to explain my chosen position, to explore the grey areas and to be fair to the other side.

Political correctness is about ideologies, freedoms, traditions, modernity, language, cultures, access, histories, inequality, standards, power and so much more.

Unfortunately, at times, movements for significant and complex social transformations have been reduced by proponents and opponents to sound bites, petty quarrels or conversely, an existential siege. PC is not an enemy operation nor a foreign, enervating, deadly disease injected into the USA or Britain by those who hate the West. It is as Western as democracy, an intrinsic part of that system that would atrophy and become dictatorial without continual contestation and disagreements.

Since time began, there have been disputative encounters between established ways and the new, between older and younger generations, between men and women, between people of various sexual orientations, between the West and the rest, between racial and ethnic majorities and minorities, and among minorities themselves, between ideas. Disruption leads to progress. The Age of Enlightenment, which transfigured European societies in the seventeenth and eighteenth centuries, became a creation myth: the way the West understands and projects itself and (less usefully) contrasts itself with other 'lesser' cultures. But the Enlightenment was not linear, and neither was it universal nor uncontroversial.

Debates raged then and continue to rage even now about the Enlightenment, the reinforcement of supremacies and the many fault lines between key thinkers and their hubristic Occidentalism. Edward Said exposes and incisively critiques these in his seminal book, *Orientalism*; proving that even now there is no clear and clean agreement among academics on that long and historic epoch.[43]

Today the incontrovertible arguments for access seem to provoke some very odd reactions. Toby Young, the right-wing journalist who turned himself into an education guru, recoils from the concept. To him inclusivity is:

> one of those ghastly, politically correct words that have survived the demise of New Labour ... [It] means wheelchair ramps, the complete works of Alice Walker in the school library (though no Mark Twain) and a Special Educational Needs Department that can cope with everything from dyslexia to Münchausen syndrome by proxy. If [then education secretary, Michael] Gove is serious about wanting to bring back O-levels, the

---

43 See the excellent essay by Kenan Malik in *The Observer*, 19 February 2017.

government will have to repeal the Equalities Act because any exam that isn't 'accessible' to a functionally illiterate troglodyte with a mental age of six will be judged to be 'elitist' and therefore forbidden by Harman's Law.[44]

I can see where he is coming from, this white, exceedingly fortunate male, whose dad got him into an Oxbridge college just by making a couple of calls.

Over many centuries, heterosexual, middle-class white men claimed most of the world's resources and decided who and what mattered. (According to some armchair geographers, Caucasians make up only 15 per cent of the world's population.) They feel they are losing status and control, which they are, but not nearly as much or as fast as they believe. Young is one of them, a man-boy with a redundant life map who needs to get a grip. But his sort will not relinquish power any time soon.

Other confrontations are also being played out.

---

44 *The Spectator*, 1 July 2012.

The third age of globalisation[45] followed the fall of the Berlin wall. Ever since then, against all expectations, economic coalescence has led to cultural disunities within countries and communities as well as between nations. Turkey, for example, an enthusiastic player in the modern marketplace, is becoming a powerhouse with 11 per cent economic growth. But the nation is bitterly split. Conservative Turks in high places are imposing their own form of political and cultural correctness. Their modernist foes are PC in the liberal sense. This contest is not as simple as it has been made out to be. Nor, really, is there a major left-wing threat to the social order. If anything, liberal democratic values are in grave danger around the world.[46] The danger comes not from PC espousers, but the raging right and nationalism.

But now for some self-reflection. No conspiracies are totally without basis. Just as all stereotypes hold some verities. There have been times when my more

---

45 The first was the age of exploration, the second the long period of European colonisation.

46 See my column 'Lazy western liberals risk being crushed by right-wing crusaders', in *International Business Times*, 9 February 2018: http://www.ibtimes.co.uk/lazy-western-liberals-risk-being-crushed-by-right-wing-crusaders-1660293

fanatical comrades have twisted, misused or misunderstood the seriousness of political correctness. There have been examples of extreme silliness and, more seriously, outrageous relativism which actually reinforced inequality or led to avoidable tragedies. Let's take the less serious examples first. When I married an Englishman in 1990, I was described as a 'bounty bar' and 'mulligatawny soup' by fellow anti-racists. (They seemed then to forget how wounding words could be.) In 1996, while on a lecture tour in New York, I used the term 'black' instead of 'African-American' and was shouted at by members of the audience. In 2016, while on a lecture tour in Pennsylvania, I inadvertently offended a few African-Americans who had decided to call themselves 'Nubians'. Their responses were, frankly, boorish. I was insulting their race and roots, they heckled. Some walked out and hissed, others stamped their feet. Three 'Nubians' later accused me of being part of a centuries-long, Western, anti-Africa conspiracy. I was born and raised in east Africa. How many of these activists know the continent?

A number of agencies, individuals and groups have,

over many years, tolerated alternative moral codes or encouraged perpetual victim status. For example, it took a very long time for the criminal justice system and social services to take seriously female genital mutilation or male victims of domestic violence. This was because of nervousness about treading into ethnic cultural zones or complicating the narrative about domestic violence. There have also been cases of PC leading to shocking outcomes. Black children have died dreadful deaths in their own homes because, it is thought, some social workers did not challenge parents and families who had their own 'cultural norms'. White girls exploited by largely Pakistani Muslim men were similarly left unprotected, because professionals wanted to ensure they were not seen as racist. This reticence still prevails when it comes to young Muslim girls who are held back, forced into marriages or genitally mutilated. It is a betrayal of the left by the left.

PC language, too, sometimes has become so fixed that it has drained words and left them pale and quivering. For instance, when mixed-race adults and children are described as 'black', and there is no room left for personal identification or nuanced identities. Why should all thespians be called 'actors'? As for the growing list of terms to describe various sexual proclivities and choices, I confess that I, too, am finding it hard to follow contemporary gender fluidities and pronoun variance. It can feel like tackling an obstacle course with a blindfold. But I will try harder, I promise. For me, the most trying and annoying aspects of new PC are the endless, judgemental tests I have to pass. In the case of Obama, for example, many African-Americans mistrusted him because a) he wasn't the descendant of slaves and b) he was raised by white people. In fact, his black Kenyan father left when he was but a boy, which made him not black enough. I myself am denounced by fellow Muslims who doubt my faith because I am married to a white, lapsed Christian and I drink wine openly, not furtively, as some of my righteous brethren do. And I am also damned as a 'traitor to my own people' by anti-racists when I criticise the practices and beliefs of some British Muslims. Worse than that, they warn me that my entirely justified criticisms embolden Islamophobes.

Feminism can be just as testing. I have had my credentials questioned because I got married (twice!), and because I sometimes use the title 'Mrs', and also because I have defended the rights of men. And this will get me into still more trouble: I really think mums expending energy on objecting blue and pink clothing for boys and or girls could be doing something more useful.

Among the most foolish PC decisions ever must surely be one made by Manchester Art Gallery. In January 2018, the gallery removed *Hylas and the Nymphs* by Victorian artist John William Waterhouse. Apparently, the rise of the #MeToo movement and the recent exposing of the President's Club prompted curators to take the artwork – which depicts naked water nymphs seducing a man – down. A statement on the gallery's website said they removed the painting to prompt a conversation: 'This gallery presents the female body as either a "passive decorative form" or a "femme fatale". Let's challenge this Victorian fantasy!'[47] I understand the provocation, and the importance of talking about the

---

47 See the report in *Manchester Evening News* by Lucy Lovell, 2 February 2018.

female form and male gaze in art, but the tactic was foolish. It got everyone in a froth over censorship. Nobody said this was easy.

All that said and fully acknowledged, the PC drive is vital, and needs to get stronger and clearer. The cause needs to be articulated assertively and also wisely. Freedom-of-speech troopers genuinely believe invisible hands are tying their tongues or gagging them, or that central and local political institutions, schools and universities, public services and the private sector are all conspiring to censor truths and protect various interest groups. They have their myths and monsters, and, luckily for them, large sections of the most powerful parts of the establishment are on side.

Are they partly right? Yes, of course. PC can feel like an affront to an individual, to traditionalist values, to a lived past. I do not want to be called a 'girl' because I am an adult, not an immature female. Would anyone call, say, the *Daily Mail* columnist, Richard Littlejohn, a 'boy'? The difference does not come out of malevolence but, more likely, thoughtlessness, or habit. Some male friends explained that it was an expression of endearment. Maybe it was. I let it go; sometimes that is the best thing to do. In a small way, I learnt that occasionally words can be tolerated even if not PC. For the greater good. It highlighted the importance of being more discerning and selective – and not to nag incessantly. More importantly, the men who call women 'girls', are products of history and society, as are all humans. Their defensiveness is a natural reaction; PC trivia can sometimes be self-defeating and brattish.

The curriculum is another issue which would benefit from more sophisticated and less emotive debates. Schools and universities have produced thousands of highly educated and successful young people. Why fix something that is not broken? Do even the most fanatic PC advocates want to rewrite what is taught on the PPE course at Oxford, or radically change the arts departments in Durham, the University of East Anglia or various London universities? Would they go further and clean up Shakespeare? These questions are important. We who are politically correct need to take them seriously, and come up with sane, rational answers. My own view is that we must be far clearer than we have been about valuing educational heritages that still have merit, in order to then provide convincing critiques of what needs to be updated and changed. Such transformations are demanding and require alliance building. Let's take slavery, which most normal people today would agree was and is evil. Black people wish to have slavery taught in all our educational establishments. Too many indigenous Britons have gone through life without ever understanding the impact of slavery on generations of black Britons, Africa or indeed on themselves at some deep level. However, if slavery is taught properly, it would be necessary to tackle the part played by black slavers and traders who were essential intermediaries in the vast and profitable Atlantic slave trade. Just as important would be to teach the history of the Arab slave trade, which predated the European business, and which continued long after abolition. I reckon such honesty would win over the most determined enemy of PC.

So, PC is flawed, and can be harmful. Despite this, its aims are noble and I still believe it has civilised discourse and made us more humane.

The Case Against Political Correctness (PC)

Culture Wars: Tradition v. Modernity, Evolutionary Advancement v. Disruptive Change

The battles between those who espouse political correctness and those who are adamantly opposed to all aspects of PC has gone on for a while. There is no resolution in sight. In the twenty-first century identity politics have gone mainstream. White, heterosexual, able-bodied middle-class and working-class men see themselves as excluded, maligned victims in the PC world. (They do have a point.) The culture war has got more bitter and aggressive. The main arguments used by the two sides, from 1980s to the present time, are listed below.

- PC violates the fundamental idea of universal, disinterested truth. As Lynne Cheney, a right-wing academic and chair of the National Endowment for the Humanities put it: 'The humanities are about more than politics, about more than social power. What gives them their abiding worth are truths that pass beyond time and circumstance; truths that, transcending accidents of class, race and gender, speak to us all.'[48]

- PC is a liberal conspiracy. Its cynical/credulous devotees seek to emasculate the nations that made them. Men and women of the left – crypto-communists – have infiltrated media, education and Academe. In conservative journals various writers have zealously argued that those young, radical students who created mayhem on campuses and elsewhere in the USA, and who opposed the war in Vietnam, came of age and took control. They are the enemy within.

- PC blasphemes against the 'Great Tradition' through cultural and knowledge relativism and has generated post-modern chaos. A guerrilla war is being fought against Western scientific and philosophical methods, rationality, secularism, and proven cultural dominance. In April 1990, for example, Roger Kimball, an editor at the conservative journal, *The New*

---

48 Lynne V. Cheney, 'Humanities in America: A Report to the President, the Congress and the American People', 1988.

Criterion, published *Tenured Radicals: How Politics Has Corrupted Our Higher Education*. Moira Weigel notes, 'Like Bloom, Kimball argued that an "assault on the canon" was taking place and that a "politics of victimhood" had paralysed universities. As evidence, he cited the existence of departments such as African American studies and women's studies.'[49] This is about envy and hatred. In higher education institutions in the US and UK, angry non-white students are becoming vocal and organised. They aim to upend the traditional syllabus and dominance of 'DWEMs', dead white european males. Everything from affirmative action and respect for diversity to gender equality policies is part of a concerted war on white men and their exceptional contributions to human development. Some white males, such as the American academic Charles Murray, have set out to 'prove' that the IQs of black Americans are lower, on average, than that of whites, and different

---

49 Weigel, *The Guardian*, op. cit.

life outcomes among racial groups are the result of genetics and inherited biological advantage.

- PC is silencing opinion. The Cato Institute, temple of libertarianism, published a report titled 'The State of Free Speech and Tolerance in America'.[50] A survey conducted for the report revealed that 58 per cent of Americans 'have political view they are afraid to share'. The percentage of timid conservatives was far higher than for liberals.

- Politically correct self-censorship 'muzzles creativity … stifles ideas, makes cowards of us all, and makes conversation boring'.[51]

- PC access to education campaigns are a threat to accumulated experience, wisdom and excellence, those of genuinely high intellect and real potential. This results in lowering standards, dumbing down.

- Equal opportunity initiatives and positive discrimination are patronising and promote men and women beyond their natural capacities. They are tokenistic to

---

50 'The State of Free Speech and Tolerance in America', Cato Institute, October 2017.
51 Daisy Waugh, *i*, 10 November 2017.

the beneficiaries and unfair to better qualified white men.

- PC protests illiberal practices. For example, when Neena Lall, the British Asian head of the country's top state primary school, tried to impose a strict uniform code that disallowed hijabs for very young girls, the left and PC lobbies launched a vicious campaign against her and forced her to back down. This shows how controlling and iniquitous political correctness has become.[52]

- PC violates a primary entitlement of citizens in liberal democracies: the right to think, speak and express themselves freely. It is invidious suppression parading as virtue. This view is held by many people from right to left. Although the right has always been militantly against any challenge to the status quo, one finds people on the left who are also defensive and protective of absolute freedoms. One of the most forthright of those was Christopher Hitchens, an impassioned leftish liberal who savaged those who

---

52 See report in *Sunday Times*, 28 January 2018.

did not buy into American liberties guaranteed by the constitution: 'There are those in the "empowerment community" who mean business about regulating speech and expression ... For the first time in American history, those who call for an extension of rights are also calling for an abridgement of speech.'[53]

- Two decades on from the Hitchens outburst, the equally fierce Claire Fox believes it is all even more oppressive now: '*Spiked*'s[54] Free Speech University Rankings 2016 show that 90 per cent of universities and students' unions censor speech ... Barely a week goes by without reports of something "offensive" being banned from campus ... this all-pervading sense of grievance, displayed by so many students, is now beginning to cause serious anguish for older commentators, who look on with horror at the increasing evidence that young people have become dangerously thin-skinned.'[55]

---

53 Op cit. pp. 137–8.
54 *Spiked* is a libertarian publication, which is written and published by ex-Marxists. Some journalists, *The Guardian*'s Suzanne Moore, for example, suspect it of alt-right tendencies. See Moore's column in *The Guardian*, 24 January 2018.
55 Claire Fox, '*I Find that Offensive!*' (Biteback, 2016), p. xvii.

- PC is an existential threat. Think of it as modern-day Stalinism, a sinister control of the human spirit and voice. Melanie Phillips says so, clearly and succinctly: '[There is] a startling abuse of power, more reminiscent practised by totalitarian regimes…'[56] Or it is Marxist or even Maoist social engineering, mind control and behaviour manipulation?

- Dictators stop free speech. The citizens of Iran, Saudi Arabia and other authoritarian regimes are brought up to know what they can and can't say. Those who defy the rules suffer terribly. The worry is that settled democracies can also be cowed. As PC spreads through societies, adults and children watch what they say and internalise the rules of acceptability. Almost without knowing it, they surrender their liberties.

- This is just simply 'mouthing the multiculturalist, identity-laden values that PC baby boomers and academic cultural relativists have been pushing for years … Is it really a victory for student power when a Con-

---

56   Melanie Phillips, 'Illiberal Liberalism', *The War of the Words*, p. 45.

servative minister orders university vice-chancellors to set up a task force to deal with the sexist "lad culture" on campus?'[57]

- If this goes on we will reduce human resilience – particularly among the young – and maniacal verbal and thought hygiene will make society unhealthy and more restive. Views which go underground start to fester and become more lethal. Trevor Phillips argues that Marine Le Pen and Trump came out of zealous political correctness.[58]

- When constrained, ideas can't grow and flower. Innovation and progress depend on individuals being unafraid risk-takers. PC will make dynamic societies dull, static, conformist and backward.

- Progressive societies should allow, indeed encourage, open debates and arguments, verbal challenges and exchanges – even with people whose ideas are abhorrent. In the twenty-first century those skills are no longer valued or practised.

- Europeans were freed from church control and

---

57 Fox, op. cit. p. 150.
58 See *Sunday Times*, 19 February 2017.

excessive restraint by Voltaire and other great thinkers of the Enlightenment. This heritage made Europe great. It must be defended and reinforced in homes, schools, colleges, universities and key institutions.

- One of my old Oxford professors with whom I fiercely debated the subject, came up with some radical new objections to PC. The intellectual mollycoddling of children and young people, he believed, would make them soft and unfit to survive the increasingly complex and competitive world. 'Do you think the Chinese worry about what words they can use to describe foreigners, or the need to be more inclusive and intolerant? India and China are unfair and unequal nations. They are also the economic powerhouses of the future.' Think about that.

The Case for Political Correctness
Change, Progress, Legitimate Claims, Power Struggles and Demonisation

- Persistent accusations of 'censorship' are unfair and used to discredit perfectly just causes. The word has lost its real meaning because it is carelessly thrown about. There is a difference between states and armies using their might to silence the voices of individuals and populations, and claims from those in the margins, people who refuse to stay in their place and demand respect and access. Suffragettes and civil rights activists were demonised in exactly this way. As Henry Miller wrote, 'The new always carries with it the sense of violation, of sacrilege … what is new, that is different, is evil, dangerous, or subversive.'[59]

- In the UK, and even in the US, land of the supposed free, state power is still used to supress open discourse and information. Official Secrets Acts do just that. In May 2011, for example, our Ministry of Defence used 'national security' as a reason to conceal the identity of an SAS man who had been charged with offences against children.[60] Edward Snowden has observed that 'The UK has just legalised the most extreme

---

59 Henry Miller, *The Air-Conditioned Nightmare* (Secker and Warburg, 1945).
60 See report in the *Telegraph*, 13 May 2011.

surveillance in the history of Western democracy. It goes further than many autocracies.'[61]

- Note that those who hate PC the most are all but silent when it comes to repressive state laws or patently unfair institutional practices. For example, free speech believers unconditionally accept our government's draconian rules on 'preventing radicalisation' in schools and universities. Speakers must be vetted, forms filled, some Muslim speakers banned because they are deemed to be undesirable or dangerous influences on young minds. Freedom of speech warriors who get vexed when students decide to give no platform to outside speakers readily acquiesce to the state. Proof, perhaps, of how their commitment to freedom of expression is conditional, and not to be trusted.

- There is also plenty of evidence of selective outrage. For example, right-wing newspapers get overexcited when university departments decide to teach black

61 Graham Vanbergen, 'The Architecture of Total Surveillance and Censorship in Britain Arrives in 2017', TruePublica, 4 January 2017: http://truepublica.org.uk/united-kingdom/architecture-total-surveillance-censorship-britain-arrives-2017/

history, yet find it perfectly 'normal' and rational that racial minorities don't get into the most prestigious universities. They are also highly indignant when nationalistic narratives are challenged. In this country it is expected that everybody should agree that what Britain did to German civilians was justifiable and that Brits alone stood out against fascism. In February 1945, UK and US dropped 3,900 tonnes of explosives on the German city of Dresden, a city with no military connections or importance. The aim of 'Operation Thunderclap', as it was known, was to kill civilians. The Allied forces were successful, and it's estimated that around 35,000 people died. Britons only want to hear about the glories and to hear over and over they beat the 'Huns'. These truths have been overlaid by patriotic political correctness; that kind of knowledge engineering is perfectly acceptable to the majority of anti-PC Britons.

- Opponents of PC are protectionists. As writer Patrick Wright observed many years ago: 'It has become a reflex sneer of the right that is no longer prepared to argue its case. However, it also has attractions for refugees from the collapsing Left, stepping out from behind all that ideological baggage to catch up with the opportunities of a world where everything seems to hang free.'

- I would go further. White lefties were fine with PC until they felt their own positions were vulnerable. When I was given a column on a newspaper, a white male journalist, who had earlier lost his, said to me bitterly: 'You got it because you were brown and female. It's bloody PC again.' I thought he was my friend.

- PC is about power: who has it, what they do with it, how they reinforce the power base, how they create fortresses and why all challenges feel to them like an invasion. Even in 2018, women and minorities are not given the chances they deserve. The PC battle goes on. The small gains made have been *because* of PC, not in spite of it.

- Literature, art, science and culture cannot stand still. Challenges and change are catalysts for human progress. What would we be without the early pioneers who did what they needed to break down barriers and enter hallowed white male spaces? Imagine no Toni Morrison, no Oscar-winning films by Steve McQueen or Turner Prize-winning art by Chris Ofili, no Sajid Javid and Sadiq Khan, no Meera Syal or Sanjeev Bhaskar. Maggie Aderin-Pocock, a black female scientist, who became co-presenter of the long-running BBC TV programme *The Sky at Night*, which had been presented for decades by Patrick Moore, a well-loved white male broadcaster. By the time of his death, the world had changed. Even the BBC realised they needed to bring in diverse talent. Could that have happened through natural evolution alone? Without campaigns and arguments? PC has always been with us, only we called it other names. Martin Luther King pushed to change language and challenge white power; Maya Angelou's lifelong fight was for respect for her people; early feminists like Gloria Steinem and Betty Friedan demanded equality and power. PC changed the world – for the better. PC is not an intellectual aberration, but part of a long struggle for equality, dignity and respect for those who have suffered exclusion and historical injustices throughout centuries.

- Anti-PC troopers claim they want untrammelled 'debate'. When we answer back (using only words) and make them uncomfortable, they try to discredit or silence us. Think of the reactions to the students in Oxford who wanted to bring down the statue of the proud white supremacist Cecil Rhodes. They put up strong reasons, debated with passion, and were denounced as 'stupid', 'illiterate' or 'insurgents'. They did not physically wreck the statue, but argued for that to happen.

- The right to free speech includes the right to react to those exercising that right. Otherwise it means individuals feeling entitled to sound off as if their points of view are sacrosanct. Saul Bellow never understood that. In 1994 he complained, 'We can't open our mouths without being denounced as racists, misogynists, supremacists, imperialists or fascists.' What he couldn't bear was that some of his careless remarks about Papuans and Zulus produced reactions beyond his warm, cosy world. Some people attacked him with words. He shouldn't have been such a snowflake. In fact, his essay about this furore is very good indeed.

I ended up on his side, but still thought those who objected had the right to do so.[62]

- Let me say this again: speech can hurt. That old adage 'sticks and stones might break your bones, but words will never hurt me' is outdated and just plain wrong. We bring our children up to care about the feelings of others; to be polite and considerate. I have never met a parent who raises her or his kids to freely express what they want. Most bullying is verbal, and disclaiming responsibility for hurtful words is indefensible. In his excellent book, the American law professor Steven J. Heyman writes, 'An individual who is subjected to degrading racial epithets feels insulted because they violate her sense of personal dignity, the speaker cannot escape responsibility for this reaction on the ground that the listener can choose to have a sense of dignity or not.'[63] He himself is white and privileged. But he gets it.

- People, creatures, nature and cultures all evolve. It's

---

62 *New York Times*, 10 March 1994.
63 Steven J. Heyman, *Free Speech and Human Dignity* (Yale University Press, 2008) p. 94.

the human story. However, the processes that lead to cultural change can, at times, be eruptive. What universities were, and what they taught in the eighteenth century, is not what they became in the nineteenth or twentieth centuries. If the deal is that some 'outsiders' will get entry as long as they accept all the norms, values, subjects and conventions, it's really no deal at all. Once you have black and Asian academics, or women in Parliament, the edifice is always going to be rocked. And a very good thing too. Education is dynamic, not static. Without new ideas and challenges to orthodoxies, it would atrophy. Even in 2018, at some of our top universities, barely any non-white political thinkers are on the reading list. Gandhi is sometimes allowed in, and occasionally Frantz Fanon, the incisive post-colonial Martinican philosopher. This is sub-standard education and is rightly being challenged.

- Free speech can be turned into a form of verbal sabotage. President Trump is the saboteur-in-chief of this movement – with backers such as Steve Bannon. As the American writer Lindy West observes with understandable concern, 'meaning is fluid. There are no standards. There are no limits. It doesn't matter what you do; it only matters what you say you do. That's how Trump can proclaim himself the "least racist person on earth" while running for president on an explicitly racist platform.'[64] This must be resisted, otherwise human communication will turn irreversibly nihilistic. PC is part of that resistance.

- Language shapes behaviour and can be as damaging as destructive acts. Sometimes the impact can be the same. When the Labour MP Owen Smith promised to 'smash [Theresa May] back on her heels', his words were blows. This is how debased our political life has become. More seriously, research carried out on political messaging by Assistant Professor Nathan Kalmoe at Louisiana State University produced some startling results. One survey group was shown ads with violent words and images, the other looked at ads that were more civil and conventional. Aggressive personality types, stimulated by the first

---

64 Lindy West, *The Guardian*, 17 January 2017.

ad, justified acts of political violence.[65] Kalmoe's conclusions should worry us all:

> Three survey experiments—including two with nationally representative samples—tested whether the mildest, most common forms of violent political rhetoric increase public support for violence against political authority, including threats against leaders, property violence, and physical violence against leaders. Together, the three studies point to the same conclusion: citizens with aggressive personality traits express greater support for violence against political authority, and their support is magnified when exposed to violent political metaphors. Interestingly, these results also show a significant opposing reaction among low-aggression citizens who expressed even lower support for violent [sic] against political authority when exposed to violent political language.[66]

---

65 See Archie Bland's piece in *The Guardian,* 31 July 2016, which looks into toxic politics and the environment that led to the murder of Jo Cox.

66 Nathan P. Kalmoe, 'Mobilizing Aggression in Mass Politics', PhD thesis, University of Michigan, 2012.

- Across our universities groups of students are calling for education that 'decolonises the mind'. About time too. As Ziauddin Sardar and Meryl Wyn Davies wrote in their brilliantly iconoclastic book on *The Satanic Verses* affair, '"Civilization as we know it" has always meant Western civilization. Civilized behaviour and products have been measured by the yardsticks of the West. Europe and now North America has always contemplated itself as the focus of the world, the axis of civilization, the goal of history, the end product of human destiny ... Colonial history and colonial Christianity did their utmost to annihilate non-Western cultures and obliterate their histories.'[67] All young people should learn a rounded and honest history. How will indigene Westerners cope in the near future, which will be determined by how well they understand other races and cultures?

- The Enlightenment is the foundational base of modernity in the West. Its ideas and wisdom spread across the globe, but several of the prophets of this

---

67 Ziauddin Sardar and Meryl Wyn Davies, *Distorted Imagination: Lessons from the Rushdie Affair* (Grey Seal Books, 1990).

transformative epoch had unsavoury views of people and lands in the south and east. J. S. Mill, Marx, Voltaire and others were men of their time, but were essentially white supremacists. Their ideas formed many of us from elsewhere. But their cultural arrogance is problematic and needs to be interrogated.

- Languages cannot be rigidly set for ever. They are organic and responsive. The most ardent conservative would not suggest we bring back words like 'nigger' into our public spaces. Words, writes Deborah Cameron, 'are constantly being inflected and re-inflected with new meaning ... It is always worth asking why, and from whose point of view, one way of using language seems obvious, natural and neutral, while another seems ludicrous, loaded and perverse.'[68]

- The Tory government wants hard-line Imams banned from speaking and has also accepted the definition of anti-Semitism to include criticism of the state of Israel. In 2017, Jo Johnson, the then Tory Universities minister, expressed severe disapproval of Israeli

---

68 Deborah Cameron, 'Words, Words, Words', in *The War of the Words*, op. cit., p. 29.

Apartheid Week, a global call out to the nation's policies and politics and, in particular, its treatment of Palestinian civilians and expansionist aims. Some Zionist groups asked their supporters to 'record, film, photograph' events, and promised to get university heads and police to stop these debates and activities.[69] Is this freedom of speech? The Brexit debates have resulted in new limits on free speech. Remainers cannot say large numbers of Brexiters were ignorant or racist or defend the 'metropolitan elite' without being savaged. Is this freedom of speech?

- As I write this, a court has ruled that UKIP and one of its MEPs, Jane Collins, have to pay substantial legal costs and damages in a defamation case brought by three MPs in Rotherham. Ms Collins had alleged Kevin Barron, John Healey and Sarah Champion knew about child victims of grooming gangs in their constituency and that they chose to do nothing. No

---

69 See aforementioned letter in *The Guardian* with hundreds of academic signatories, including many British Jews, on this new and worrying development, 27 February 2017.

irrepressible defenders of freedom have questioned the judgment or denounced it as 'censorship'.[70]

- Anti-political correctness is today's orthodoxy, a trope that wins one friends in high places and ensures establishment respect. Always suspect guys who tell you how stupidly PC they were at university and how they saw the light. What they saw was, in fact, easy gain and reputational enhancement as they marched rightwards and shed their previous skins.

- Its enemies slander it, but the aims of PC are serious and honourable. When judges are all white, from the same background and of an age, justice suffers. When the BBC pays its female star presenters far less than male equivalents, it breaks the law, offends the principles of equality, wounds it reputation and betrays its mission. When gay people want their history to be told, it is to seek redress for past neglect and discrimination, and to claim pride and place in the national narratives. When crude, rude and nasty language is

---

70 See report in *The Independent*, 16 February 2018.

disallowed in the public space, we all breathe cleaner air. All these are examples of PC in practice.

- PC is, as the late Lisa Jardine (one of Britain's greatest public intellectuals) used to say, about 'enlarging horizons'. All her life she argued that diversities liven up inert aspects of culture and makes us alert to differences and new possibilities in a fast-changing world.

- In spite of being incessantly savaged, PC has led to kinder and more respectful interactions. Remember when, in 2011, David Cameron told Angela Eagle to 'calm down, dear'? A large number of female MPs felt he had revealed his inner sexism, and he was forced to apologise. In 2018, Henry Bolton was to stand down as leader of UKIP, because his young mistress sent vile, racist texts to a friend about Meghan Markle. All hell broke loose. Even the *Mail* and UKIP sorts were offended. It seems we are all PC now.

- People of influence in the media, academe, politics, business and so on, tell us over and over again that debates and rational discourse allow people to learn and change their minds. Trevor Phillips writes, 'I was brought up with the notion that you win arguments only with superior knowledge. Yet it seems that all too many of our students – and their teachers – no longer share that view.'[71] Too right, arguments simply entrench positions. Does Phillips, a black man, really believe that all Martin Luther King had to do was to engage racists and white supremacists in civilised debate to win civil rights?

• Writer Ellie Mae O'Hagan makes important observations about the enemies of PC and their collaborators:

> What is happening here is threefold: first, the right is so accustomed to its values dominating public discourse that many people within it have become grown-up babies who can't bear to live in a society that isn't constantly pandering to their sensitivities … Second, others on the right are shrewdly exploiting the important principle of freedom of speech to ensure their ideas are the prevailing ones in society, by claiming any challenge to them as oppression. And finally, these groups are being aided and

---

71 Trevor Phillips, 'Students flee reality, and the far right rises', *Sunday Times*, 19 February 2017.

abetted by liberal dupes and cowardly university institutions, both of which are convinced that they're engaged in an impartial debate about Enlightenment values that isn't actually taking place.[72]

- We are told 'everyone is afraid to say what they think'. Yeah right. We can see how scared Katie Hopkins, Nigel Farage and Richard Littlejohn are. And how the always-furious who ring up radio stations to rage against 'multiculturalism', Muslims, women and the left are forced to hide what they really, really think. I am daily subjected to the rage of white men who hate me being in the public space, hate me because I am brown, articulate, on the left, a feminist, antiracist and resolutely PC. They sometimes try to get me disinvited from speaking events. Sometimes they succeed.

- The right to offend and hurt is not absolute. To provoke and insult Muslims is really not an essential duty even for libertarians. Ever since the Rushdie

---

72 *The Guardian*, 27 February 2017.

crisis, those who pride themselves on being un-PC
bait Muslims just because they can. Richard Dawkins,
the legendary scientist, is one of them. In July 2018
he tweeted that though an atheist, he found church
bells so much nicer than 'aggressive sounding' Muslim
calls to prayer. This inevitably hurt many Muslims,
including myself. He had his fun and moment of
superiority.[73]

- In the US and UK, the right have repeatedly criticised or tried to stop subversive art. Vice-President
Mike Pence, for example, was apoplectic when the
black cast of the hit show *Hamilton* spoke up on
stage about black lives and American values. Trump
tweeted: 'Our wonderful future V.P Mike Pence was
harassed last night at the theater by the cast of *Hamilton*, cameras blazing. This should not happen!' He
went on to say, 'The Theater must always be a safe
and special place. The cast of *Hamilton* was very rude
last night to a very good man, Mike Pence. Apolo-
gize!' One of the actors, Brandon Victor Dixon, later

---

73 Kaya Burgess, 'Outcry after Richard Dawkins criticises Muslim call to prayer',
The Times, 18 July 2018.

responded to Trump by tweeting, 'Conversation is not harassment sir. And I appreciate Mike Pence for stopping to listen.'[74]

74 *Hollywood Reporter*, 18 November 2016.

Part III

How to Live a PC Life in this Age of Alt-Right, Brexit, Culture Wars and Tribalism

To RECAP THE arguments I have made thus far, I practise and defend political correctness because vehement enemies of the concept and movement are fouling the human environment. The new barbarians are pitiless. Two occurrences prompted me to write this book, one domestic, one international; one small, one momentous. At Middlesex University, where I teach, during a session on censorship and freedom at a literary festival, a bright, young female Muslim student asked whether in this free world, she was free to object to absolute freedom of speech. A tutor humiliated her. A guest speaker called her 'stupid'. She burst into tears.

The second prompt was the election campaign of Donald Trump. When Fox news anchor Megyn Kelly asked him, 'You've called women you don't like "fat pigs", "dogs", "slobs" and "disgusting animals". You once told a contestant on *Celebrity Apprentice* it would be a "pretty picture" to see her on her knees.' He hit back: 'I don't frankly have time for total political correctness. And to be honest with you, this country doesn't have time, either.' He was right. When he maligned Muslims and Mexicans, including Mexican US district judge Gonzalo Curiel, he gained more supporters. Attacking PC proved to be a winning strategy. So he carries on. And so, he will win again. We PC idealists can either stand up and fight or surrender before the forces of darkness.

Since the 1980s, PC has pushed through bold, overdue and radical cultural shifts in the arts, popular culture, politics and power, ideas and actual practice.

Some of us will keep fighting the fight, hold up the flag of political correctness, carry on with integrity, intelligence and reflection. We are not always right, not above the law, not beyond fair criticism, and should never be purveyors of absolute certainties. We have a difficult and essential job to do in this tempestuous age of culture conflicts and war of the words.

When anything can be said and done, you get Donald Trump, Steve Bannon, Nigel Farage, Katie Hopkins and British-born Milo Yiannopoulos (the worst of the lot). He 'propelled the alt-right movement into the mainstream,' says Heidi Beirich, who directs the Intelligence Project at the Southern Poverty Law Center, which tracks hate groups and the hard right. Beirich says she's not even sure if Yiannopoulos believes in the alt-right's tenets or just found a juvenile way to mix internet culture and extreme ideology to get attention. 'It's like he's joking: "Ha ha, let me popularize the worst ideas that ever existed,"' she says. 'That's new, and that's scary.'[75]

In February 2017, handsome and swaggering Yiannopoulos, crashed down to earth. By this time he had

---

75 Joel Stein, 'Milo Yiannopoulos Is the Pretty, Monstrous Face of the Alt-Right', Bloomberg, 15 September 2016: https://www.bloomberg.com/features/2016-america-divided/milo-yiannopoulos/

been banned from Twitter for life and had had some university talks cancelled. Like Icarus, he had flown too close to the sun. Or maybe he was more a Narcissus, lethally consumed by himself. The man who had turned himself into a global brand and was praised by his adopted 'daddy' Trump, made a big mistake. On a video he appeared to approve of sex between sexually aware thirteen-year-olds and older men. He knew this because he had done it, he said breezily. This was too much, even for his own band of free speech crazies. He had to resign from his job as senior editor of the hard-right Breitbart website. Humbled, he explained that he was touched inappropriately by two men when he was a child. To his former self, such justifications ('victimhood') would have been contemptible. Ah well, poor Milo has learnt that there is no such thing as absolute freedom of speech. We may disagree about where the lines should be, but lines there are, personal and political, about what we can or can't say in public spaces.

We PC idealists will not be directed by fundamentalist libertarians to think and talk like them. If they really believe in their credo, they must accept contestation not cowardly surrender.

Two thirds of Britons believe offence is too easily felt by diverse citizens and half say they are 'not allowed' to say what they think about issues. According to Tom Clark, support for the 'politically incorrect is higher among under 25-year-olds than older people. For older people, including pensioners, there is – if anything – more support for taking care with language.'[76] This is what pollsters found in early 2018. In the same survey, 45 per cent of respondents preferred 'politicians who spoke bluntly, without worrying about who they offend,' against 38 per cent who prefer a leader who 'spoke carefully' to avoid 'unnecessarily offending people'. Populist leaders will be rubbing their hands with glee. Group thinking leads to group shrieking. Too many adults internalise the views of others because of social pressures or because they trust charismatic dissemblers, or because they are uninformed or just plain lazy. They are then easily manipulated by the powerful.

---

76 YouGov/Prospect poll. See article by Tom Clark in *The Guardian*, 16 February 2018. See also *Prospect* for full research evidence.

In 2016 and 2017, several key politicians 'bravely' took on migrants, liberal values, national identity and multiculturalism. Channelling Enoch Powell, Labour's Rachel Reeves blamed migrants – doctors, builders, nurses, cleaners and carers, among others – for various national tribulations, and for causing an 'explosive' environment around the country. Tory Amber Rudd meanwhile accused companies of betraying British workers by taking on foreign staff. Oxford Professor Joshua Silver, a physicist, has said that Ms Rudd's phraseology reminded him of the tone of Adolf Hitler's autobiography *Mein Kampf*: 'Some of our senior politicians speak about foreigners in a way … which is almost designed to make this tolerant nation less tolerant towards foreigners.' He contacted West Midlands Police after reading press coverage of the speech and consulting a draft of it, as well as monitoring the 'feedback' it generated online.[77] Britain has become a coarse, frightening, cruel place because politicians have become populist and irresponsible.

---

77 *Daily Mail*, 12 January 2017.

Nigel Farage is a folk hero in white heartlands because he speaks as he feels. His anti-PC persona persuaded millions to vote for Brexit. Stan, one of my neighbours, was one of them. 'British people were happy to keep to old ways. I mean why should I care about these men becoming women or no good Arabs? Who cares about me? And why can't I have golliwogs?' Stan has a Filipino carer. At an arts event, a theatre director from a northern town declared PC was 'a sinister conspiracy against the real people of England who finally spoke out during the referendum'. Newspapers, TV and radio programmes are becoming uncontrollable and aggressively non-PC.

Institutions that promoted racial and gender equality are moribund. Reports of racist, sexist and homophobic abuse and attacks are increasing. People of colour and women are terrorised by online desperados. Perpetrators feel no shame; they feel themselves to be the real oppressed victims of egalitarian battalions. The hard right is marching again. MP Jo Cox was brutally murdered by a neo-fascist who remains unrepentant. Almost a third of referrals to government anti-radicalisation programmes are now for right-wing extremists.[78] Alarmingly, many of these are young children.

Am I disheartened? Do I feel PC is now burnt toast? No. Such surveys are interesting, but crude indicators which aim, I think, to explain why the terribly disgruntled, genuinely excluded and intolerant rose up during the run-up to Brexit and the last American election. Remember, however, that other polls have shown that most young people voted against Brexit and Trump, and they are instinctively politically correct and inclusive. The young are entitled to fashion their own values and question everything about the world they are slowly inheriting. May they have the courage to continue to do so.

Populism is a real force across the world, but a vast array of other forces are ranged against it, too. I sense a change in the air. Brendan O'Neill, editor of *Spiked* magazine, ideologically close to Claire Fox and other free expression absolutists, found his inner PC pixie in 2016 when a new version of the film

---

78 *The Guardian*, 20 June 2017.

Ghostbusters was released. One of its stars, Leslie Jones, black and female, was horribly reviled online. O'Neill responded,

> Jones is a very funny African-American comedian and the only good thing in the otherwise flat, weird and mirth-free Ghostbusters reboot. Yet for the past 48 hours she has been subjected to vile racist abuse by alt-right tweeters and gamers and other assorted saddos for her part in what they view as the feministic crime of remaking Ghostbusters with a female cast. She has left Twitter. This might mark the moment when the alt-right went full racist, full berserk, full unhinged.[79]

This is a man who hates PC, and yet felt moved to protect a black female star from barbarians. Thank you, Brendan.

In 2016, I wrote a column in *The Guardian* arguing for more courageous and judicious political correctness. In my view:

---

79 *The Spectator*, 20 July 2016.

> US journalists, politicians and public intellectuals are engaged in impassioned debates about the balance between inviolable liberties and social obligations, diversity claims and national unity. Their British equivalents have been lackadaisical, more acquiescent. The forces of conservatism and petty nationalism have triumphed and are pursuing minority rights and progressive values.[80]

The response to the opinion piece was extraordinarily vituperative even for these shrill and noisy times when all dissent is seen as a crime against the nation and 'the people'. However, when good, honest, ethical men and women come to believe that political correctness can lead to the politics of fragmentation, they must be heeded not disparaged. I happen to think they are right, up to a point. Demagoguery is found among the politically correct as well as the politically incorrect.

If we are to convince more people of the value of these changes, we, espousers of political correctness, will have

---

80 *The Guardian*, 8 November 2016.

to be more principled and less defensive than perhaps has been the case in the past. PC is not about hiding inconvenient truths about, say, absent black fathers, destructive feminists, reactionary Islam, or dysfunctional white working-class families. Relativism helps no one. When individuals and communities are overprotected or expect to behave as they wish because of discrimination or injustice they have faced, problems fester and scrutiny is seen as invasive. That leaves victims of internal oppression without protection or redress and encourages criminality. The mainly Pakistani grooming gangs which pursued and exploited young white girls, many troubled and lost, show what can happen when some citizens feel they are not bound by societal morals and the nation's laws. For me, PC is about universal values, a single template. I use the same criteria when assessing situations or making judgements on behaviours. If we make excuses for miscreants and wrongdoers because they come from groups that are discriminated against, we become appeasers.

In this grave new world, internet users are getting madder and more brazen. Their unruliness has spread, fouling real human interactions. Furthermore, Islamicist violence is making liberal forbearance seem like pathetic weakness. Globalisation and reckless capitalism, mass migration from unfamiliar lands and the loss of old ways are all causing disorientation and a surge in self-pity. According to Professor Jonathan Haidt of New York University, social justice activists are also to blame. The 'accusatory and vindictive approach of many social activists and diversity trainers may actually have increased the desire and willingness of some white men to say and do un-PC things'.[81]

A more disturbing accusation is that we who are PC are responsible for the rise of the new hard-right in the West, comprising racial purists, nationalists, the economically deprived, macho men and disillusioned mainstream conservatives. Are these accusers serious or knowingly malevolent? Are feminists then responsible for turning some men into vicious rapists? And do we blame Germany's Chancellor Merkel for neo-

---

81 *New York Times*, 1 June 2016.

fascist revivalism because she did her Christian duty by accepting a million asylum seekers? Some of those refugees turned out bad and gave the hard-right exactly what they needed. Those criminals must be held to account and rightly condemned.[82] They hurt the host nation and all the displaced peoples who are desperate for asylum. But these crimes were then used to justify fascism. Moral opprobrium was *entirely* rerouted to Merkel and refugee malfeasants who are responsible for a surge in crimes since 2015. This is right-wing moral relativism at its worst.

Political correctness may, at times, have gone a little crazy. But anti-political correctness has now become seriously and dangerously mad, bad and treacherous. For its exponents to feel safe in it, the world had to keep its recognisable shape, rhythm, polarities, power structure, modes of communication and

---

82 See, for example, *Daily Telegraph* report on 15 August 2016 on how rapes committed by a group of refugees were used by hard-right parties to discredit Merkel and turn people against her.

gradations, gatekeepers, understood standards and settled realities.

Here is one of the most pathetic examples of defensive thinking. In March 2018, the BBC launched an ambitious and spectacular series, *Civilisations*. It paid homage to patrician Kenneth Clarke's groundbreaking *Civilisation*, which was first aired in the late '60s, while also boldly subverting the style and focus of the original programme. A number of white, male critics were discomfited by the diversity of the panel. Such roles were previously automatically handed over to patrician, white Oxbridge men.[83]

But back to the meaning and purpose of political correctness. Is it a movement for equality and access to power? Yes. Does it seek to overturn previous controllers of politics and culture? Yes again, but not violently. Is it about policing language? No. It's about balancing free speech with social responsibility.

Let's talk about trolls, the extremists of free speech. They verbally abuse, demean, threaten and offend people

---

83 James Marriott, 'BBC has missed the point of civilisation', *The Times*, 19 February 2018.

because they can, and because they are protected by anonymity. Britons and Americans of all shades, from left to right, are increasingly concerned about amoral internet giants, and verbal and pictorial nihilism online. Concerned citizens are beginning to understand the perils of absolute free speech. They are subconsciously becoming more politically correct. Responding to the growing concern, Facebook started to secretly moderate content using mysterious guidelines.[84] You could say PC is steadily going mainstream. In July 2017, the BBC was found to be operating a pay policy of gross discrimination against females and people of colour. Few Britons thought the disparities were just competitive market forces. There was moral outrage. Welcome to PC in action.

There have also been delicious examples of hypocrisy. Peter Thiel is a Trump-backing Silicon Valley multimillionaire and absolute libertarian. Gawker was a money-making website that invaded the privacy of individuals and 'exposed' their sexual and other secrets.

---

84 See the special report in *The Guardian*, 22 May 2017.

Thiel was furious with the website for outing him as a gay man. He used his money to back a successful legal action against Gawker brought by Hulk Hogan, a former professional boxer. Gawker lost and was sunk. The libertarian Thiel had his limits. Freedom was not a free for all.[85]

There is a growing consensus, a new understanding that when anything goes, everything that is worthwhile and important to human existence, goes too. Mutuality, restraint, empathy, decency, safety, care, justice and dignity are being swept away in the interconnected globe. Millions now see that, and are agitating for regulation and accountability. Politicians and people want the internet giants to take more responsibility for the content on their sites. I believe that libertarians are rattled by these demands. Political correctness has never been more important. Our time has come. Let's be less fanatical; more strategic, smarter and more effective than we have been.

---

[85] See *Conspiracy* by Ryan Holiday (Profile Books, 2018) and the excellent review by John Arlidge in *The Times*, 4 March 2018.

A Brief Guide on How to Be Principled and Politically Correct

1. Do not be cowed by the tidal waves of abuse, fakery and barney that wash up when political correctness sets off yet another cultural squall. Examine the issue. Come to a considered view, decide whether you can defend PC in this instance and then stick there.

2. No more feeble squirming. Stand up for what's right and necessary, for principles.

3. PC is not a religion. It does not require swearing blind faith to its premises. You can oppose some forms of PC; opt out of some campaigns.

4. You are more likely to unsettle the adamantly un-politically correct if you are honest.

5. When you are taking on anti-PC foes, remember to be considerate and use PC language. Communication skills will help immeasurably.

6. Always ask your assailants if they think they are entitled to hurt and affront people whenever they choose. I do when the time is right. 'So your freedom of speech gives you the right to hurt, frighten and demean me does it? Do I have that same right when,

say, it comes to your children and mother? Why does it give you so much satisfaction, this right to offend?'

7. Use all the brilliant examples of PC actually changing the world. *Vogue* always saw itself as a publication by and for rich white people. Diversity was barely a whisper in its corridors. Then a black man, Edward Enninful, became editor and did the PC thing. *Vogue* got colour. The #MeToo movement and Black Lives Matter show the potential and power of PC.

8. Choose your battles. You can't take them all up. It can wear you out, and, at times, break you. The power of the other side is overwhelming. Also remember that you are not enlisting in some army which expects you to act without questioning. PC is all about challenges including challenges to itself.

9. Beware of PC righteousness.

10. The clever thing to do is to extend the repertoire of PC and include those who resent it. A large number of young men are lost and inwardly deeply troubled. Feminists should campaign for them. PC is about equality for all. It really should not be about avenging past injustices, exclusions and cabals.

11. Go on PC/Anti-PC dates. Go to nice places where you can talk about why the world needs shaking up. Mentor young people who are PC and who are finding it hard.

12. Maybe we need a rebranding, or a second wave PC movement. But the term is so misrepresented, contaminated and toxic, maybe we should rebrand it 'PP' – public politeness. Surely even old fogeys and right-wing bullies would buy into that?

13. Use the complaints systems intelligently. If newspapers and broadcasters misrepresent, say, the student campaigns to decolonise the syllabus – as they have done – complain to the paper or to the broadcaster or regulatory bodies. Miqdaad Versi, a Muslim activist, for example, is making a name for himself by demanding and getting corrections, even in the right-wing tabloids.[86]

14. You need like-minded friends. When I get mercilessly attacked for pointing out racism, I surround myself with people who can reassure and comfort

---

86 See his article in *The Guardian*, 23 January 2017.

me. This is a culture war which can wound and disable the strongest of us.

15. Remind sceptics of how attitudes have been transformed by political correctness. Every time a politician or another public figure has to apologise for saying the wrong thing, claim this as a PC victory.

The last word goes to Andrew Marr; here we have a perfect definition and defence of the aims of political correctness, articulated by a privileged, white, male public intellectual:

> Personally, as a 58-year-old white male in a good job, I find all this – proselytising vegetarianism, #MeToo, hostility to the old British Empire, much more fluid attitudes to gender and a nagging anxiety about the climate – unsettling and even threatening. But social change is about these subtle, relentless, restless changes that are happening all around us all the time. In the end this is called history.
>
> It's what makes being alive in 2018 so interesting.[87]

---

87 *Evening Standard*, 2 March 2018.